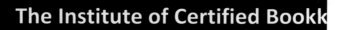 The Institute of Certified Bookkeepers

Level II

CERTIFICATE IN MANUAL BOOKKEEPING

REVISION KIT

British Library Cataloguing-in-Publication Data

A catalogue record for this book is available from the British Library.

Published by:

Kaplan Publishing UK
Unit 2 The Business Centre
Molly Millars Lane
Wokingham
RG41 2QZ

ISBN 978-0-85732-780-2

© Kaplan Financial Limited, 2012

Printed and bound in Great Britain

All rights reserved. No part of this publication may be reproduced, stored in a retrieval system, or transmitted, in any form or by any means, electronic, mechanical, photocopying, recording or otherwise, without the prior written permission of Kaplan Publishing.

The text in this material and any others made available by any Kaplan Group company does not amount to advice on a particular matter and should not be taken as such. No reliance should be placed on the content as the basis for any investment or other decision or in connection with any advice given to third parties. Please consult your appropriate professional adviser as necessary. Kaplan Publishing Limited and all other Kaplan group companies expressly disclaim all liability to any person in respect of any losses or other claims, whether direct, indirect, incidental, consequential or otherwise arising in relation to the use of such materials.

INDEX TO QUESTIONS AND ANSWERS

	Page number	
	Question	**Answers**
ACCOUNTING FOR VAT	1	71
THE CASH BOOK AND THE PETTY CASH BOOK	10	80
BANK RECONCILIATION STATEMENTS	21	86
CONTROL ACCOUNTS AND RECONCILIATIONS OF THE SALES AND PURCHASE LEDGER ACCOUNTS	34	98
CORRECTION OF ERRORS AND THE SUSPENSE ACCOUNT	40	104
DEPRECIATION OF FIXED ASSETS	48	108
ACCRUALS AND PREPAYMENTS	54	117
BAD DEBTS	59	123
FINAL ACCOUNTS OF A SOLE TRADER	62	126

Workbook Preface

This workbook has been written for the Level II Certificate in Manual Bookkeeping of the Institute of Certified Bookkeepers (ICB).

It is designed to complement the corresponding ICB study text which contains the detailed syllabus coverage.

Section 1

PRACTICE QUESTIONS

ACCOUNTING FOR VAT

1   VAT RELATED TERMS

The following are commonly used VAT related terms:

- Output tax
- Input tax
- Zero rated item
- Exempt item
- Standard rated
- Tax point

Required:

Define each of the above terms.

2   ERIN

Erin is registered for VAT. During May, she sells goods with a tax exclusive price of £600 to Kyle on credit. As Kyle is buying a large quantity of goods, Erin reduces the price by 5%. She also offers a discount of another 3% if Kyle pays within 10 days. Kyle does not pay within the 10 days.

VAT is charged at the standard rate of 20%.

(a)   How much VAT should be charged on this transaction?

(b)   What is the total amount that Kyle will pay to Erin?

3 LAUREL

At 1 December 20X5, Laurel owes the HMRC VAT of £23,778. During the month of December, she recorded the following transactions:

- Sales of £800,000 exclusive of VAT at the standard rate.
- Purchases of £603,360 inclusive of VAT at the standard rate.

Required:

Complete Laurel's VAT control account for the quarter ended 31 December 20X5.

VAT Control Account

	£		£

4 SALES AND PURCHASES

If sales (inclusive of VAT) amounted to £27,612.50, and purchases (excluding VAT) amounted to £18,000.

(a) What would be the balance on the VAT account, assuming all items are subject to tax at 20%?

£ ☐

(b) Is this balance due to or from HMRC?

5 RAMSGATE

A summary of the transactions of Ramsgate, who is registered for VAT at 20%, shows the following for the month of August 20X9.

- Outputs £60,000 (exclusive of tax)
- Inputs £40,286 (inclusive of tax)

At the beginning of the month Ramsgate owed £3,400 to HMRC, and during the month he has paid £2,600 to them.

Required:

Complete Ramsgate's VAT control account for the month ended 31 August 20X9.

VAT Control Account

	£		£

6 LAKER

Laker returned goods to their supplier that had a net value of £200. What entries are required to record this transaction if VAT is payable at 20%?

Account name	Amount £	Debit ✓	Credit ✓

7 Which of the following statements are true?

1 VAT is a form of indirect taxation.
2 If input tax exceeds output tax the difference is payable to the authorities.
3 VAT is included in the reported sales and purchases of the business.
4 VAT cannot be recovered on some purchases.

A 1 and 4
B 1 and 2
C 2 and 3
D 3 and 4

8 DUNCAN BYE

You are a self-employed bookkeeper and Duncan Bye, a motor engineer, is one of your clients. He is registered for VAT with registration number 131 7250 19.

His records for the quarter ended 30 June 20X1 showed the following:

Sales day book

	Gross £	Net £	VAT £
April	8,100.00	6,750.00	1,350.00
May	7,812.00	6,510.00	1,302.00
June	9,888.00	8,240.00	1,648.00
	25,800.00	21,500.00	4,300.00

Purchases day book

	Gross	Net	VAT
	£	£	£
April	3,780.00	3,150.00	630.00
May	3,924.00	3,270.00	654.00
June	3,216.00	2,680.00	536.00
	10,920.00	9,100.00	1,820.00

He also gives you some details of petty cash expenditure in the quarter.

	£
Net purchases	75.60
VAT	15.12
	90.72

He informs you that he used some parts on a job to repair his own car. The parts had previously cost him £120 (exclusive of VAT).

Required:

Prepare the following VAT form for the period, ready for Duncan Bye's signature.

PRACTICE QUESTIONS: SECTION 1

Value Added Tax Return

For the period

HM Customs and Excise

Duncan Bye
Low House
Low Green
Derbyshire
DE1 7XU

140784/06

Your VAT Office telephone number is 0151 644211

For Official Use

Registration number | Period 06 X1

You could be liable to a financial penalty if your completed return and all the VAT payable are not received by the due date.

Due date: 31.07.X1

For official use

ATTENTION

If you may trade or pay taxes in euro from Jan 1999, Contact your Business Advice Centre for C&E queries or Treasury Enquiry Unit on 020 7270 4558

Before you fill in this form read the notes on the back and the VAT leaflet *'Filling in your VAT Return'*. Fill in all boxes clearly in ink, and write 'none' where necessary. Don't put a dash or leave any box blank. If there are no pence write '00' in the pence column. **Do not** enter more than one amount in any box.

For official use			£	p
	VAT due in this period on **sales** and other outputs	1		
	VAT due in this period on **acquisitions** from other **EC Member States**	2		
	Total VAT due (**the sum of boxes 1 and 2**)	3		
	VAT reclaimed in this period on **purchases** and other inputs (including acquisitions from the EC)	4		
	Net VAT to be paid to Customs or reclaimed by you (Difference between boxes 3 and 4)	5		
	Total value of **sales** and all other outputs excluding any VAT. **Include your box 8 figure.**	6		00
	Total value of **purchases** and all other inputs excluding any VAT. **Include your box 9 figure.**	7		00
	Total value of all **supplies** of goods and related services, excl any VAT, to other **EC Member States**.	8		00
	Total value of all **acquisitions** of goods and related servs, excl any VAT, from other **EC Member States**.	9		00

Retail schemes. If you have used any of the schemes in the period covered by this return, enter the relevant letter(s) in this box.

If you are enclosing a payment please tick this box.

DECLARATION: You, or someone on your behalf, must sign below.
I, ... declare that the
(Full name of signatory in BLOCK LETTERS)
information given above is true and complete.
Signature... Date .... 20..............
A false declaration can result in prosecution.

VAT 100 (Full)   PCU (June 1996)

9 MARK AMBROSE

Your work involves bookkeeping and accounting services mainly to small businesses.

One of your clients is Mark Ambrose, a self-employed master joiner. A summary of his day books for the quarter ended 30 September 20X1 is included below.

Sales day book

	Work done £	VAT £	Total £
July	12,900.00	2,580.00	15,480.00
August	13,200.00	2,640.00	15,840.00
September	12,300.00	2,460.00	14,760.00
	38,400.00	7,680.00	46,080.00

Purchase day book

	Net £	VAT £	Total £
July	5,250.00	1,050.00	6,300.00
August	5,470.00	1,094.00	6,564.00
September	5,750.00	1,150.00	6,900.00
	16,470.00	3,294.00	19,764.00

Petty cash expenditure for quarter (VAT inclusive)

July	£108.00
August	£96.00
September	£120.00
	324.00

I have also used some materials from my stock, valued at £500 (exclusive of VAT), to repair my garage roof.

Bad debts list – 30 September 20X1

Date	Customer	Total (including VAT)
30 November 20X0	High Melton Farms	£300.00
3 January 20X1	Concorde Motors	£180.00
4 April 20X1	Bawtry Engineering	£120.00

These have now been written off as bad debts.

Required:

Prepare the following VAT form for the period, ready for Mark Ambrose's signature.

PRACTICE QUESTIONS: SECTION 1

HM Customs and Excise

Value Added Tax Return
For the period

Mark Ambrose
High Park House
High Melton
Doncaster
DN5 7EZ

Your VAT Office telephone number is 0151 644211

For Official Use

Registration number: 123 9872 17
Period: 09 X1

You could be liable to a financial penalty if your completed return and all the VAT payable are not received by the due date.

Due date: 31.10.X1

For official use

ATTENTION

If you may trade or pay taxes in euro from Jan 1999, Contact your Business Advice Centre for C&E queries or Treasury Enquiry Unit on 020 7270 4558

Before you fill in this form read the notes on the back and the VAT leaflet *'Filling in your VAT Return'*. Fill in all boxes clearly in ink, and write 'none' where necessary. Don't put a dash or leave any box blank. If there are no pence write '00' in the pence column. **Do not** enter more than one amount in any box.

For official use			£	p
	VAT due in this period on **sales** and other outputs	1		
	VAT due in this period on **acquisitions** from other **EC Member States**	2		
	Total VAT due (**the sum of boxes 1 and 2**)	3		
	VAT reclaimed in this period on **purchases** and other inputs (including acquisitions from the EC)	4		
	Net VAT to be paid to Customs or reclaimed by you (Difference between boxes 3 and 4)	5		
	Total value of **sales** and all other outputs excluding any VAT. **Include your box 8 figure.**	6		00
	Total value of **purchases** and all other inputs excluding any VAT. **Include your box 9 figure.**	7		00
	Total value of all **supplies** of goods and related services, excl any VAT, to other **EC Member States**.	8		00
	Total value of all **acquisitions** of goods and related servs, excl any VAT, from other **EC Member States**.	9		00
	Retail schemes. If you have used any of the schemes in the period covered by this return, enter the relevant letter(s) in this box.			

If you are enclosing a payment please tick this box.

DECLARATION: You, or someone on your behalf, must sign below.
I, ... declare that the
(Full name of signatory in BLOCK LETTERS)
information given above is true and complete.
Signature.. Date .... 20.............
A false declaration can result in prosecution.

0141846
VAT 100 (Full)   PCU (June 1996)

LEVEL II: CERTIFICATE IN MANUAL BOOKKEEPING

10 SIMON WHITE ACCOUNTANCY

You work for Simon White Accountancy. Your work includes bookkeeping and accounting services to small businesses, particularly small hotels and guesthouses, restaurants and public houses.

One of your clients is Crescent Hotel which has 40 bedrooms, a small restaurant and bar. The hotel is owned by John and Norma Thistle. You have been given some books and records relating to the quarter ended 30 September 20X1.

Summary of day books for quarter ended 30 September 20X1

Sales day book

	Net £	VAT £	Gross £
July	17,300.00	3,460.00	20,760.00
August	20,200.00	4,040.00	24,240.00
September	17,600.00	3,520.00	21,120.00

Sales – Gross takings in cash

	Bar £	Restaurant £
July	3,960.00	7,020.00
August	5,040.00	6,780.00
September	3,540.00	6,300.00

Purchase day book

	Net £	VAT £	Gross £
July }	5,190.00	1,038.00	6,228.00
August } Hotel	6,060.00	1,212.00	7,272.00
September }	5,280.00	1,056.00	6,336.00
July – September (bar and restaurant)	10,800.00	2,160.00	12,960.00

Petty cash expenditure

Gross for period: £481.75

NOTE

To: Simon

From: John

Date: 16 October 20X1

Simon, you are aware that we had three residents last year (December 20X0) from a company working in the area. This company has now gone into liquidation and we have been informed that we will not receive any funds against this debt. Could you please, if possible, claim back the VAT from HMRC.

The gross value of the invoice was £600.00.

Also, in mid-August it was Norma's birthday and we 'put on' a surprise party for her. We used £300 worth of stock from the restaurant and the bar.

Do we need to adjust any figures for VAT?

Required:

Prepare the following VAT form for the period on behalf of Crescent Hotels.

PRACTICE QUESTIONS: SECTION 1

HM Customs and Excise

Value Added Tax Return

For the period 01/07/X1 to 30/09/X1

John Thistle
t/as Crescent Hotel
High Street
Whitby
YO21 37L   140784/06

Your VAT Office telephone number is 0151 644211

For Official Use

Registration number: 179 6421 27
Period: 09 X1

You could be liable to a financial penalty if your completed return and all the VAT payable are not received by the due date.

Due date: 31.10.X1

For official use

ATTENTION

If you may trade or pay taxes in euro from Jan 1999, Contact your Business Advice Centre for C&E queries or Treasury Enquiry Unit on 020 7270 4558

Before you fill in this form read the notes on the back and the VAT leaflet *'Filling in your VAT Return'*. Fill in all boxes clearly in ink, and write 'none' where necessary. Don't put a dash or leave any box blank. If there are no pence write '00' in the pence column. **Do not** enter more than one amount in any box.

For official use			£	P
	VAT due in this period on **sales** and other outputs	1		
	VAT due in this period on **acquisitions** from other **EC Member States**	2		
	Total VAT due (**the sum of boxes 1 and 2**)	3		
	VAT reclaimed in this period on **purchases** and other inputs (including acquisitions from the EC)	4		
	Net VAT to be paid to Customs or reclaimed by you (Difference between boxes 3 and 4)	5		
	Total value of **sales** and all other outputs excluding any VAT. **Include your box 8 figure.**	6		00
	Total value of **purchases** and all other inputs excluding any VAT. **Include your box 9 figure.**	7		00
	Total value of all **supplies** of goods and related services, excl any VAT, to other **EC Member States.**	8		00
	Total value of all **acquisitions** of goods and related servs, excl any VAT, from other **EC Member States.**	9		00

Retail schemes. If you have used any of the schemes in the period covered by this return, enter the relevant letter(s) in this box.

If you are enclosing a payment please tick this box.

DECLARATION: You, or someone on your behalf, must sign below.
I, ... declare that the
(Full name of signatory in BLOCK LETTERS)
information given above is true and complete.
Signature.. Date .... 20.............

A false declaration can result in prosecution.

0141846
VAT 100 (Full)   PCU (June 1996)   F

THE CASH BOOK AND THE PETTY CASH BOOK

11 HICKORY HOUSE

Hickory House maintains a petty cash book as a book of prime entry. The following transactions all took place on 31 Dec and have been entered in the petty cash-book as shown below. No entries have yet been made in the general/main ledger.

Petty cash-book

Date	Details	Amount	Date	Details	Amount	VAT	Postage	Motor expenses	Office expenses
20XX		£	20XX		£	£	£	£	£
31 Dec	Bal b/d	210.00	31 Dec	Stapler	6.72	1.12			5.60
31 Dec	Bank	90.00	31 Dec	Stamps	15.00		15.00		
			31 Dec	Parking	14.88	2.48		12.40	
			31 Dec	Stationery	19.20	3.20			16.00
			31 Dec	Bal c/d	244.20				
		300.00			300.00	6.80	15.00	12.40	21.60

What will be the double entry required to record this in the general/main ledger?

Account name	Amount £	Debit ✓	Credit ✓

12 MESSI & CO

Messi & Co maintains a petty cash book as a book of prime entry. The following transactions all took place on 31 Dec and have been entered in the petty cash-book as shown below. No entries have yet been made in the general/main ledger.

Petty cash-book

Date	Details	Amount	Date	Details	Amount	VAT	Postage	Motor expenses	Office expenses
20XX		£	20XX		£	£	£	£	£
31 Dec	Op bal.	100.00	31 Dec	Paper	27.33	4.55			22.78
			31 Dec	Stamps	4.50		4.50		
			31 Dec	Biscuits	6.60	1.10			5.50
			31 Dec	Parking	9.60	1.60		8.00	
			31 Dec	Cl bal.	51.97				
		100.00			100.00	7.25	4.50	8.00	28.28

What will be the double entry required to record this in the general/main ledger?

Account name	Amount £	Debit ✓	Credit ✓

13 PETTY CASH

Two amounts have been paid from petty cash:

- Envelopes for £14.00 excluding VAT
- Motor Fuel for £24 including VAT

(a) Complete the petty cash vouchers below.

Petty cash voucher	
Date:	7.07.XX
Number:	PC256
Envelopes	
Net	£
VAT	£
Gross	£

Petty cash voucher	
Date:	7.07.XX
Number:	PC257
Motor Fuel	
Net	£
VAT	£
Gross	£

Part way through the month the petty cash account had a balance of £145.00. The cash in the petty cash box was checked and the following notes and coins were there.

Notes and coins	£
4 × £20 notes	80.00
1 × £10 notes	10.00
2 × £5 notes	10.00
12 × £1 coins	12.00
40 × 50p coins	20.00
45 × 20p coins	9.00

(b) Reconcile the cash amount in the petty cash box with the balance on the petty cash account.

Amount in petty cash box	£
Balance on petty cash account	£
Difference	£

(c) At the end of the month the cash in the petty cash box was £27.25

Complete the petty cash reimbursement document below to restore the imprest amount of £150.

Petty cash reimbursement	
Date: 31.07.20XX Amount required to restore the cash in the petty cash box.	£

14 THE ARCHES

This is a summary of petty cash payments made by The Arches.

Mick's Motors paid	£20.00 (no VAT – exempt)
Stamps paid	£19.00 (no VAT – exempt)
Office Essentials paid	£22.00 (net of VAT)

(a) Enter the above transactions, in the order in which they are shown, in the petty cash-book below.

(b) Total the petty cash-book and show the balance carried down.

Petty cash-book

Debit side		Credit side					
Details	Amount £	Details	Amount £	VAT £	Postage £	Travel £	Stationery £
Bal. b/d	200.00						

15 PETTY CASH VOUCHERS

Given below are the petty cash vouchers that have been paid during the week ending 12 January 20X1 out of a petty cash box run on an imprest system of £150 per week. At the end of each week a cheque requisition is drawn up for a cheque for cash to bring the petty cash box back to the imprest amount.

Voucher no	Amount £	Reason
03526	13.68	Postage
03527	25.00	Staff welfare
03528	14.80	Stationery (including £2.46 VAT)
03529	12.00	Taxi fare (including £2.00 VAT)
03530	6.40	Staff welfare
03531	12.57	Postage
03532	6.80	Rail fare
03533	7.99	Stationery (including £1.33 VAT)
03534	18.80	Taxi fare (including £3.13 VAT)

Required:

(a) write up the petty cash book given;

(b) prepare the cheque requisition for the cash required to restore the petty cash box to the imprest amount;

(c) post the petty cash book totals to the main ledger accounts given.

Petty cash book											
Receipts			**Payments**								
Date	Detail	Total	Date	Detail	Voucher no	Total	Postage	Staff welfare	Stationery	Travel	VAT
		£				£	£	£	£	£	£

CHEQUE REQUISITION FORM

CHEQUE DETAILS

Date ....

Payee ....

Amount £ ....

Reason ....

Invoice no. (attached/to follow) ....

Receipt (attached/to follow) ....

Required by   (Print) ....

                  (Signature) ....

Authorised by: ....

Main ledger accounts

Postage account

		£			£
5 Jan	Balance b/d	248.68			

Staff welfare account

		£			£
5 Jan	Balance b/d	225.47			

Stationery account

		£			£
5 Jan	Balance b/d	176.57			

Travel expenses account

		£			£
5 Jan	Balance b/d	160.90			

VAT account

		£			£
			5 Jan	Balance b/d	2,385.78

16 IMPREST SYSTEM

A business runs its petty cash on an imprest system with an imprest amount of £100 per week.

At the end of the week ending 22 May 20X1 the vouchers in the petty cash box were:

Voucher no	£
02634	13.73
02635	8.91
02636	10.57
02637	3.21
02638	11.30
02639	14.66

The cash remaining in the petty cash box was made up as follows:

£10 note	1
£5 note	2
£2 coin	3
£1 coin	7
50p coin	5
20p coin	4
10p coin	1
5p coin	2
2p coin	3
1p coin	6

You are required to reconcile the petty cash in the box to the vouchers in the box at 22 May 20X1 and if it does not reconcile to suggest reasons for the difference.

17 IMPREST SYSTEM (2)

A business runs an imprest system with an imprest amount of £120. The rules of the petty cash system are as follows:

- only amounts of less than £30 can be paid out of petty cash, any larger claims must be dealt with by filling out a cheque requisition form
- all petty cash claims over £5 must be supported by a receipt or invoice
- the exception to this is that rail fares can be reimbursed without a receipt provided that the petty cash voucher is authorised by the department head
- all other valid petty cash vouchers can be authorised by you, the petty cashier
- all petty cash vouchers that are authorised are given a sequential number.

You have on your desk 10 petty cash vouchers which have been completed and you must decide which can be paid and which cannot.

PETTY CASH VOUCHER				
Authorised by	Claimed by J Athersych		No	
Date	Description		Amount	
15/3/X1	Coffee		4	83
	Milk		1	42
	Biscuits		0	79
		Total	7	04
(Receipt is attached)				

PETTY CASH VOUCHER				
Authorised by	Claimed by J Athersych		No	
Date	Description		Amount	
15/3/X1	Envelopes		4	85
		Total	4	85
(No receipt)				

PETTY CASH VOUCHER				
Authorised by Department Head		Claimed by F Rivers	No	
Date	Description		Amount	
16/3/X1	Rail fare		12	80
		Total	12	80
(No receipt)				

PETTY CASH VOUCHER				
Authorised by		Claimed by M Patterson	No	
Date	Description		Amount	
16/3/X1	Computer discs		4	20
	Printer paper		2	40
		Total	6	60
(No receipt)				

PETTY CASH VOUCHER				
Authorised by		Claimed by D R Ray	No	
Date	Description		Amount	
17/3/X1	Lunch – entertaining clients		42	80
		Total	42	80
(Bill attached)				

PETTY CASH VOUCHER				
Authorised by	Claimed by J Athersych	No		
Date	Description		Amount	
17/3/X1	Milk		1	42
	Tea bags		2	28
		Total	3	70

(No receipt)

PETTY CASH VOUCHER				
Authorised by	Claimed by D R Ray	No		
Date	Description		Amount	
18/3/X1	Rail fare		12	50
		Total	12	50

(No receipt)

PETTY CASH VOUCHER				
Authorised by	Claimed by M Patterson	No		
Date	Description		Amount	
18/3/X1	Special delivery postage		19	50
		Total	19	50

(Receipt attached)

PETTY CASH VOUCHER				
Authorised by	Claimed by M T Noble	No		
Date	Description		Amount	
18/3/X1	Ink for printer		17	46
		Total	17	46

(Receipt attached)

PETTY CASH VOUCHER				
Authorised by	Claimed by J Norman	No		
Date	Description		Amount	
18/3/X1	Rail fare		7	60
		Total	7	60

(No receipt)

18 IMPREST SYSTEM (3)

A business runs its petty cash system on an imprest system with an imprest amount of £100 per week. During the week ended 30 April 20X1 the following petty cash vouchers were paid:

Voucher no	Amount £	Reason
002534	4.68	Coffee/milk
002535	13.26	Postage
002536	10.27	Stationery (including £1.71 VAT)
002537	15.00	Taxi fare (including £2.50 VAT)
002538	6.75	Postage
002539	7.40	Train fare
002540	3.86	Stationery (including £0.64 VAT)

Required:

- **write up these vouchers in the petty cash book given;**
- **post the totals of the petty cash book to the main ledger accounts given.**

Petty cash book											
Receipts			**Payments**								
Date	Detail	Total	Date	Detail	Voucher no	Total	Postage	Stationery	Tea & coffee	Travel	VAT
		£				£	£	£	£	£	£

Main ledger accounts

Postage account

	£		£
23 April Balance b/d	231.67		

Stationery account

	£		£
23 April Balance b/d	334.78		

Tea and coffee account

	£		£
23 April Balance b/d	55.36		

Travel expenses account

	£		£
23 April Balance b/d	579.03		

VAT account

	£		£
		23 April Balance b/d	967.44

PRACTICE QUESTIONS: SECTION 1

BANK RECONCILIATION STATEMENTS

19 RIVERS LTD

On 28 June Rivers Ltd received the following bank statement as at 23 June.

Remember: assume today's date is 30 June unless told otherwise.

Midway Bank PLC
52 The Parade, Middleton, MD1 9LA

To: Rivers Ltd   Account No 28012877   23 June 20XX

Statement of Account

Date 20XX	Detail	Paid out £	Paid in £	Balance £	
04 June	Balance b/f			3,115	C
04 June	Cheque 101013	650		2,465	C
04 June	Cheque 101014	1,420		1,045	C
05 June	Cheque 101015	60		985	C
07 June	Cheque 101018	450		535	C
12 June	Bank Giro Credit Ayreshire build		970	1,505	C
13 June	Cheque 101016	615		890	C
15 June	Direct Debit COLLINS	175		715	C
20 June	Direct Debit Rent	500		215	C
23 June	Bank Interest		15	230	C
23 June	Bank Charges	20		210	C
23 June	Paid in at Midway Bank		300	510	C

D = Debit   C = Credit

The cash book as at 23 June is shown below.

Cash book

Date	Details	Bank	Date	Cheque number	Details	Bank
20XX		£	20XX			£
01 June	Balance b/f	3,115	01 June	111013	Indigo Beds	650
17 June	Bracken Ltd	300	01 June	111014	DirectFit	1,420
21 June	Airfleet Interiors	560	01 June	111015	Langdon	60
22 June	Harris Homes	333	02 June	111016	QPF Ltd	615
			03 June	111017	OMD Ltd	815
			03 June	111018	Hamden Ltd	450
			15 June	111019	Freeman and Cope	522
			15 June		COLLINS	175

KAPLAN PUBLISHING

(a) Check the items on the bank statement against the items in the cash book.

(b) Enter any items in the cash book as needed.

(c) Total the cash book and clearly show the balance carried down at 23 June (closing balance) and brought down at 24 June (opening balance).

(d) Complete the bank reconciliation statement as at 23 June.

Note: Do not make any entries in the shaded boxes.

Bank reconciliation statement as at 23 June 20XX

Balance per bank statement	£
Add:	
Name:	£
Name:	£
Total to add	£
Less:	
Name:	£
Name:	£
Total to subtract	£
Balance as per cash book	£

20 LUXURY BATHROOMS

On 28 April Luxury Bathrooms received the following bank statement as at 24 April.

Remember: assume today's date is 30 April unless told otherwise.

SKB Bank plc
68 London Road, Reading, RG8 4RN

To: Luxury Bathrooms   Account No: 55548921   24 April 20XX

Statement of Account

Date 20XX	Detail	Paid out £	Paid in £	Balance £	
03 April	Balance b/f			17,845	C
03 April	Cheque 120045	8,850		8,995	C
04 April	Bank Giro Ricketts & Co		465	9,460	C
04 April	Cheque 120046	2,250		7,210	C
05 April	Cheque 120047	64		7,146	C
08 April	Cheque 120048	3,256		3,890	C
14 April	Direct Debit AMB Ltd	2,265		1,625	C
14 April	Direct Debit D Draper	2,950		1,325	D
14 April	Cheque 120050	655		1,980	D
22 April	Paid in at SKB Bank		2,150	170	C
22 April	Bank charges	63		107	C
23 April	Overdraft fee	25		82	C

D = Debit   C = Credit

PRACTICE QUESTIONS: SECTION 1

The cash book as at 24 April is shown below.

Cash Book

Date	Details	Bank £	Date	Cheque	Details	Bank £
01 April	Balance b/f	17,845	01 April	120045	R Sterling Ltd	8,850
19 April	Olsen & Lane	2,150	01 April	120046	Bert Cooper	2,250
22 April	Frith Ltd	685	01 April	120047	Hetko & Sons	64
22 April	Hodgetts & Co	282	02 April	120048	Barrett Ltd	3,256
			02 April	120049	K Plomer	542
			08 April	120050	I&E Brown	655
			08 April	120051	T Roberts	1,698
			14 April		AMB Ltd	2,265

(a) Check the items on the bank statement against the items in the cash book.

(b) Enter any items in the cash book as needed.

(c) Total the cash book and clearly show the balance carried down at 24 April (closing balance) and brought down at 25 April (opening balance).

(d) Complete the bank reconciliation statement as at 24 April.

Note: Do not make any entries in the shaded boxes.

Bank reconciliation statement as at 24 April 20XX.

Balance per bank statement	£
Add:	
Name:	£
Name:	£
Total to add	£
Less:	
Name:	£
Name:	£
Total to subtract	£
Balance as per cash book	£

KAPLAN PUBLISHING

21 BANK RECONCILIATION (1)

The bank statement has been compared with the cash book and the following differences identified:

1 Bank interest paid of £82 was not entered in the cash book.

2 A cheque paid for £450 has been incorrectly entered in the cash book as £540.

3 Cheques totalling £1,980 paid into the bank at the end of the month are not showing on the bank statement.

4 A BACS receipt of £1,750 from a customer has not been entered in the cash book.

The balance showing on the bank statement is a credit of £5,250 and the balance in the cash book is a debit of £5,472.

Use the following table to show the THREE adjustments you need to make to the cash book.

Adjustment	Amount £	Debit/Credit

22 BANK RECONCILIATION (2)

Given below are the cash receipts book, cash payments book and bank statement for a business for the week ending 11 March 20X1.

Required:

- Compare the bank statement to the cash book.

- Correct the cash receipts and payments books for any items which are unmatched on the bank statement.

- Total the cash receipts book and cash payments book.

- Find the balance on the cash book if the opening balance on 7 March was £860.40 cash in hand.

- Explain why the amended cash book balance and the bank statement balance at 11 March are different.

PRACTICE QUESTIONS: SECTION 1

Cash receipts book

Date	Narrative	Total £	VAT £	Debtors £	Other £	Discount £
20X1						
7/3	Paying in slip 0062	1,147.45	90.05	583.52	450.28	23.60
8/3	Paying in slip 0063	1,086.41	68.84	643.34	344.22	30.01
9/3	Paying in slip 0064	1,332.01	81.37	809.59	406.85	34.20
10/3	Paying in slip 0065	1,012.95	57.02	652.76	285.14	18.03
11/3	Paying in slip 0066	1,158.46	59.24	779.88	296.22	23.12

Cash payments book

Date	Details	Cheque No	Code	Total £	VAT £	Creditors £	Cash purchases £	Other £	Discount received £
20X1									
7/3	P Barn	012379	PL06	383.21		383.21			
	Purchases	012380	ML	274.04	45.67		228.37		
	R Trevor	012381	PL12	496.80		496.80			6.30
8/3	F Nunn	012382	PL07	218.32		218.32			
	F Taylor	012383	PL09	467.28		467.28			9.34
	C Cook	012384	PL10	301.40		301.40			
9/3	L White	012385	PL17	222.61		222.61			
	Purchases	012386	ML	275.13	45.85		229.28		
	T Finn	012387	PL02	148.60		148.60			
10/3	S Penn	012388	PL16	489.23		489.23			7.41
11/3	P Price	012389	PL20	299.99		299.99			
	Purchases	012390	ML	270.12	45.02		225.10		

KAPLAN PUBLISHING

Bank statement

FINANCIAL BANK plc   CONFIDENTIAL

You can bank on us!

10 Yorkshire Street Account   CURRENT   Sheet 00614
Headingley   Account name T R FABER LTD
Leeds LS1 1QT
Telephone: 0113 633061

Statement date   11 March 20X1   Account Number 27943316

Date	Details	Withdrawals (£)	Deposits (£)	Balance (£)
7/3	Balance from sheet 00613			860.40
	Bank giro credit L Fernley		406.90	1,267.30
9/3	Cheque 012380	274.04		
	Cheque 012381	496.80		
	Credit 0062		1,147.45	1,643.91
10/3	Cheque 012383	467.28		
	Cheque 012384	301.40		
	Credit 0063		1,086.41	
	SO – Loan Finance	200.00		1,761.64
11/3	Cheque 012379	383.21		
	Cheque 012386	275.13		
	Cheque 012387	148.60		
	Credit 0064		1,332.01	
	Bank interest		6.83	2,293.54

SO	Standing order	DD	Direct debit	CP	Card purchase
AC	Automated cash	OD	Overdrawn	TR	Transfer

23 BANK RECONCILIATION (3)

Given below is the cash book of a business and the bank statement for the week ending 20 April 20X1.

Required:

Compare the cash book to the bank statement and note any differences that you find.

Cash book

Receipts		£	Payments		£
16/4	Donald & Co	225.47	16/4	Balance b/d	310.45
17/4	Harper Ltd	305.68	17/4	Cheque 03621	204.56
	Fisler Partners	104.67	18/4	Cheque 03622	150.46
18/4	Denver Ltd	279.57	19/4	Cheque 03623	100.80
19/4	Gerald Bros	310.45		Cheque 03624	158.67
20/4	Johnson & Co	97.68	20/4	Cheque 03625	224.67
			20/4	Balance c/d	173.91
		1,323.52			1,323.52

EXPRESS BANK   CONFIDENTIAL

You can bank on us!

High Street
Fenbury
TL4 6JY
Telephone: 0169 422130

Account: CURRENT
Account name: P L DERBY LTD
Sheet 0213

Statement date: 20 April 20X1
Account Number: 40429107

Date	Details	Withdrawals (£)	Deposits (£)	Balance (£)
16/4	Balance from sheet 0212			310.45 OD
17/4	DD – District Council	183.60		494.05 OD
18/4	Credit		225.47	268.58 OD
19/4	Credit		104.67	
	Cheque 03621	240.56		
	Bank interest	3.64		408.11 OD
20/4	Credit		305.68	
	Credit		279.57	
	Cheque 03622	150.46		
	Cheque 03624	158.67		131.99 OD

| SO | Standing order | DD | Direct debit | CP | Card purchase |
| AC | Automated cash | OD | Overdrawn | TR | Transfer |

24 GRAHAM

The cash account of Graham showed a debit balance of £204 on 31 March 20X3. A comparison with the bank statements revealed the following:

			£
1	Cheques drawn but not presented		3,168
2	Amounts paid into the bank but not credited		723
3	Entries in the bank statements not recorded in the cash account		
	(i)	Standing orders	35
	(ii)	Interest on bank deposit account	18
	(iii)	Bank charges	14
4	Balance on the bank statement at 31 March		2,618

Required:

(a) **Show the appropriate adjustments required in the cash account of Graham bringing down the correct balance at 31 March 20X3.**

(b) **Prepare a bank reconciliation statement at that date.**

25 KIVETON CLEANING

Data

The following are the cash book and bank statements of Kiveton Cleaning.

Receipts June 20X1

CASH BOOK – JUNE 20X1				CB 117
Date	Details	Total	Sales ledger control	Other
1 June	Balance b/d	7,100.45		
8 June	Cash and cheques	3,200.25	3,200.25	–
15 June	Cash and cheques	4,100.75	4,100.75	–
23 June	Cash and cheques	2,900.30	2,900.30	–
30 June	Cash and cheques	6,910.25	6,910.25	–
		£24,212.00	£17,111.55	

Payments June 20X1

Date	Payee	Cheque no	Total	Purchase ledger control	Operating overhead	Admin overhead	Other
1 June	Hawsker Chemical	116	6,212.00	6,212.00			
7 June	Wales Supplies	117	3,100.00	3,100.00			
15 June	Wages and salaries	118	2,500.00		1,250.00	1,250.00	
16 June	Drawings	119	1,500.00				1,500.00
18 June	Blyth Chemical	120	5,150.00	5,150.00			
25 June	Whitby Cleaning Machines	121	538.00	538.00			
28 June	York Chemicals	122	212.00	212.00			
			£19,212.00	£15,212.00	£1,250.00	£1,250.00	£1,500.00

Crescent Bank plc
High Street
Sheffield

Statement no: 721

Page 1

Account: Alison Robb t/a Kiveton Cleaning
Account no: 57246661

Date	Details	Payments £	Receipts £	Balance £
20X1				
1 June	Balance b/fwd			8,456.45
1 June	113	115.00		8,341.45
1 June	114	591.00		7,750.45
1 June	115	650.00		7,100.45
4 June	116	6,212.00		888.45
8 June	CC		3,200.25	4,088.70
11 June	117	3,100.00		988.70
15 June	CC		4,100.75	5,089.45
15 June	118	2,500.00		2,589.45
16 June	119	1,500.00		1,089.45
23 June	120	5,150.00		4,060.55 O/D
23 June	CC		2,900.30	1,160.25 O/D

Key:	S/O	Standing Order		DD	Direct Debit
	CC	Cash and cheques		CHGS	Charges
	BACS	Bankers automated clearing		O/D	Overdrawn

Required:

Examine the business cash book and the business bank statement shown in the data provided above. Prepare a bank reconciliation statement as at 30 June 20X1. Set out your reconciliation in the proforma below.

Proforma

BANK RECONCILIATION STATEMENT AS AT 30 JUNE 20X1

£

Balance per bank statement

Outstanding lodgements:

Unpresented cheques:

Balance per cash book   £

26 NATURAL PRODUCTS LTD

You are the cashier at Natural Products Ltd, a manufacturer of cosmetics. Your duties include writing up the cash book.

Today is 6 July 20X1.

(a) Total the receipts and payments side of the cash book and determine the balance on the cash account if the balance at the start of the week was £84,579.77 in hand.

(b) Post the totals of the cash receipts book and cash payments book to the main ledger accounts given.

(c) Compare the cash book to the bank statement.

Take each item on the bank statement and then tick it when it is agreed to a cash book entry – also tick the cash book entry. Any cheques earlier than 389 will remain unticked on the bank statement in this example as the cash payments book does not go far enough back. (In practice these would be agreed to earlier pages in the cash payments book and therefore ticked.)

Cash book receipts

Date	Narrative	Paying in Slip	Total	Debtors	Mail order	VAT control	Discount allowed
26/6	Trade debtors	598	15,685.23	15,685.23			
	Mail order (Chq/PO)	599	394.51		328.76	65.75	
	Mail order (CC)	600	91.71		76.43	15.28	
27/6	Trade debtors	601	6,650.28	6,650.28			
	Mail order	602	118.45		98.71	19.74	
	Megastores plc	CHAPS	11,755.25	11,755.25			204.17
28/6	Trade debtors	603	12,223.81	12,223.81			
	Mail order	604	622.18		518.49	103.69	
29/6	Trade debtors	605	5,395.40	5,395.40			
	Mail order	606	100.69		83.91	16.78	
30/6	Trade debtors	607	2,641.68	2,641.68			
	Mail Order/shop	608	254.91		212.43	42.48	
29/6	Freeman Foods Group	CHAPS	14,776.04	14,776.04			256.64
30/6	Totals						

Cash book payments

Date	Narrative	Cheque	Total	Creditors	Salaries	Other	VAT control	Discount received
26/6	Blackwood Foodstuffs	389	325.99	325.99				
	Bruning & Soler	390	683.85	683.85				
	Dehlavi Kosmetatos	391	2,112.16	2,112.16				
	Environmentally Friendly Co Ltd	392	705.77	705.77				
	Greig Handling (Import)	393	1,253.98	1,253.98				
	Halpern Freedman	394	338.11	338.11				
	Kobo Design Studio	395	500.00	500.00				
	Rayner Food Co	396	375.22	375.22				
	Year 2000 Produce Co	397	1,100.68	1,100.68				
27/6	HM Customs & Excise	398	23,599.28				23,599.28	
28/6	Salaries - Bank Giro	400	48,995.63		48,995.63			
30/6	Arthur Chong Ltd	401	235.55	235.55				
	Dwyer & Co (Import)	402	469.55	469.55				23.48
	Earthworld Ltd	403	449.28	449.28				22.46
	English Electricity	DD	163.17			135.98	27.19	
	English Telecom	DD	229.24			191.04	38.20	
	Totals							

Main ledger accounts

Sales ledger control account

		£			£
24/6	Balance b/d	312,465.99			

Mail order sales account

		£			£
			24/6	Balance b/d	26,578.46

VAT control account

		£			£
			24/6	Balance b/d	29,375.32

Discount allowed account

		£			£
24/6	Balance b/d	4,627.56			

Purchases ledger control account

		£			£
			24/6	Balance b/d	25,476.34

Salaries account

		£			£
24/6	Balance b/d	105,374.36			

Electricity account

		£			£
24/6	Balance b/d	1,496.57			

Telephone account

		£			£
24/6	Balance b/d	967.47			

Discount received account

		£			£
			24/6	Balance b/d	336.58

FINANCIAL BANK PLC

CONFIDENTIAL

You can bank on us!

467 HIGH STREET TAUNTON TA1 9WE	Account	CURRENT	Sheet	455
	Account name		NATURAL PRODUCTS LIMITED	

Telephone 01832 722098

20X1 Statement date: 30 JUNE 20X1 Account Number 34786695

Date	Details		Withdrawals (£)	Deposits (£)	Balance (£)
27 JUN	Balance from sheet 454				11,305.11
27 JUN	MEGASTORES PLC	CHAPS		11,755.25	
	COUNTER CREDIT 591			13,604.01	
	COUNTER CREDIT 592			112.13	
	374		127.09		
	376		5,955.80		
	ENGLISH ELECTRIC	DD	163.17		30,530.44
28 JUN	COUNTER CREDIT 593			11,655.24	
	COUNTER CREDIT 594			683.11	
	COUNTER CREDIT 595			112.19	
	372		87.93		
	389		325.99		
	ENGLISH TELECOM	DD	229.24		42,337.82
29 JUN	COUNTER CREDIT 596			325.11	
	COUNTER CREDIT 597			60,331.90	
	391		2,112.16		
	382		331.80		
	FREEMAN FOODS GRP	CHAPS		14,776.04	
	COUNTER CREDIT 598			15,685.23	
	COUNTER CREDIT 599			394.51	
	COUNTER CREDIT 600			91.71	
	394		338.11		
	395		500.00		
	386		441.09		
	388		111.94		130,107.22
30 JUN	COUNTER CREDIT 601			6,650.28	
	COUNTER CREDIT 602			118.45	
	381		117.54		
	384		3,785.60		
	387		785.11		
	390		683.85		
	393		1,253.98		
	399		175.10		
	COUNTER CREDIT 603			12,223.81	
	COUNTER CREDIT 604			622.18	142,920.76

key   SO Standing order   DD Direct debit   CP Card purchase   AC Automated cash   OD Overdrawn
CHAPS Clearing House Automated Payments System   BACS Bankers Automated Clearing Service

CONTROL ACCOUNTS AND RECONCILIATIONS OF THE SALES AND PURCHASE LEDGER ACCOUNTS

27 FINAL ACCOUNTS

You are working on the final accounts of a business (ignore VAT)

You have the following information:

(a) A payment of £4,185 to a supplier has been credited to the supplier's account in the purchases ledger.

(b) A supplier with a balance of £2,170 has been listed as £2,710.

(c) A credit purchase of £750 has not been included in the relevant supplier's account in the purchase ledger.

(d) A casting error has been made and one of the supplier accounts has been undercast by £462.

(e) A supplier account with a balance of £1,902 has been omitted from the list.

(f) Purchase returns totalling £540 has been entered twice in error.

You now need to make the appropriate adjustments in the table below. For each adjustment clearly state the amount and whether the item should be added or subtracted from purchase ledger.

	Add/Subtract	£
Total from list of balances		52,750
Adjustment for (a)		
Adjustment for (b)		
Adjustment for (c)		
Adjustment for (d)		
Adjustment for (e)		
Adjustment for (f)		
Revised total to agree with PLCA		47,494

28 FINAL ACCOUNTS (2)

You are working on the final accounts of a business (ignore VAT).

You have the following information:

(a) A casting error has been made and one of the customer accounts has been overcast by £73.

(b) Sales returns totalling £280 has been entered twice in error.

(c) A receipt of £2,771 from a customer has been debited to the customer's account in the sales ledger.

(d) A credit sale of £3,090 has not been included in the relevant customer's account in the sales ledger.

(e) A customer account with a balance of £935 has been omitted from the list.

(f) A customer with a balance of £4,725 has been listed as £4,275.

You now need to make the appropriate adjustments in the table below. For each adjustment clearly state the amount and whether the item should be added or subtracted from the sales ledger.

	Add/Subtract	£
Total from list of balances		31,820
Adjustment for (a)		
Adjustment for (b)		
Adjustment for (c)		
Adjustment for (d)		
Adjustment for (e)		
Adjustment for (f)		
Revised total to agree with SLCA		30,960

29 BASIL SPENCE

Basil Spence is a dealer in fancy goods. At 1 January 20X9 his ledger included the following balances.

	£
Debtors	17,349
Creditors	16,593

The debtors at 1 January 20X9 were as follows:

	£
N Pevsner	5,700
R Hackney	5,823
The Prince of Wales Hotel	5,826

The creditors at 1 January 20X9 were as follows:

	£
E Lutyens	5,481
M Hutchinson	5,553
H Falkner	5,559

During January 20X9 Basil's books of prime entry showed the following:

Purchases day book	£	Sales day book	£
Lutyens	2,850	Pevsner	150
Hutchinson	2,055	Hackney	5,280
Falkner	3,360	Prince of Wales Hotel	4,995
	8,265		10,425

Cash payments book	£	Cash receipts book	£
Lutyens	2,700	Hackney	5,700
Hutchinson	150	Prince of Wales Hotel	5,826
Falkner	2,469		
	5,319		11,526

Hackney argued about £123 of his outstanding balance, saying that the goods concerned were of the wrong design. Basil decided to write off this amount.

Required:

For the month of January 20X9, write up the:

(a) individual debtors' and creditors' accounts;

(b) sales ledger and purchases ledger control accounts;

(c) bad debt expense account;

(d) individual debtors' and creditors' listings.

30   BOOKS OF A BUSINESS

The following totals are taken from the books of a business:

		£
1 January 20X1	Credit balance on purchases ledger control account	5,926
	Debit balance on sales ledger control account	10,268
31 January 20X1	Credit sales	71,504
	Credit purchases	47,713
	Cash received from credit customers	69,872
	Cash paid to creditors	47,028
	Sales ledger balances written off as bad	96
	Sales returns	358
	Purchases returns	202
	Discounts allowed	1,435
	Discounts received	867
	Contra entry	75

Required:

(a) **Prepare the purchases ledger control account and balance at the end of the month.**

(b) **Prepare the sales ledger control account and balance at the end of the month.**

31 BIRKETT

The purchases ledger control account of Birkett is as follows:

Purchases ledger control account

	£		£
Purchase returns	13,418	Balance b/f	84,346
Cash book	525,938	Purchases (purchases	
Balance c/f	97,186	day book)	552,196
	_____		_____
	636,542		636,542
	_____		_____
		Balance b/f	97,186

Balances extracted from the purchases ledger totalled £96,238.

The following errors have been discovered.

1. The purchases day book was undercast by £6,000.
2. A cash account total of £10,858 was posted to the control account as £9,058.
3. A credit balance of £1,386 on the purchases ledger had been set off against a sales ledger debit balance but no entry had been made in the control accounts (a contra entry).
4. A debit balance of £40 in the list of purchases ledger balances had been extracted as a credit balance.
5. A credit balance of £3,842 had been omitted from the list of balances.

Required:

(a) Correct the control account.

(b) Reconcile the adjusted account with the sum of the balances extracted.

32 ROBIN & CO

The balance on the sales ledger control account of Robin & Co on 30 September 20X0 amounted to £3,825 which did not agree with the net total of the list of sales ledger balances at that date of £3,362.

The errors discovered were as follows:

1. Debit balances in the sales ledger, amounting to £103, had been omitted from the list of balances.
2. A bad debt amounting to £400 had been written off in the sales ledger but had not been posted to the bad debts expense account or entered in the control accounts.
3. An item of goods sold to Sparrow, £250, had been entered once in the sales day book but posted to his account twice.

4   No entry had been made in the control account in respect of the transfer of a debit of £70 from Quail's account in the sales ledger to his account in the purchases ledger (a contra entry).

5   The discount allowed column in the cash account had been undercast by £140.

Required:

(a)   Make the necessary adjustments in the sales ledger control account and bring down the balance.

(b)   Show the adjustments to the net total of the original list of balances to reconcile with the amended balance on the sales ledger control account.

33 ERRORS

When carrying out the sales ledger control account reconciliation the following errors were discovered:

(a)   a bad debt of £800 had been written off in the subsidiary ledger but not in the main ledger;

(b)   a contra entry of £240 had been made in the subsidiary ledger but not in the main ledger;

(c)   the discount allowed column in the cash receipts book had been undercast by £100.

Required:

Produce journal entries to correct each of these errors.

Account	Amount £	Debit ✓	Credit ✓

Account	Amount £	Debit ✓	Credit ✓

Account	Amount £	Debit ✓	Credit ✓

34 PURCHASES LEDGER CONTROL ACCOUNT

When carrying out the purchases ledger control account reconciliation the following errors were discovered:

(a) the purchases day book was overcast by £1,000;

(b) the total of the discount received column in the cash payments book was posted to the main ledger as £89 instead of £98;

(c) a contra entry of £300 had been entered in the subsidiary ledger but not in the main ledger.

Required:

Produce journal entries to correct each of these errors.

Account	Amount £	Debit ✓	Credit ✓

Account	Amount £	Debit ✓	Credit ✓

Account	Amount £	Debit ✓	Credit ✓

CORRECTION OF ERRORS AND THE SUSPENSE ACCOUNT

35 PERCY

You are working on the final accounts of your friend Percy's business with a year-end of 31 December. A trial balance has been drawn up and a suspense account opened with a debit balance of £9,630. You need to make some corrections and adjustments for the year ended 31 December 20X1.

Record the journal entries needed in the general ledger to deal with the items below. You do not need to give narrative.

You should remove any incorrect entries, where appropriate, and post the correct entries.

(a) Two customers have been identified as having serious cash flow problems. Borrett Ltd owes £500 and hasn't made any payments for 6 months. Abbott & Co owes £715 and Percy has received notice of their liquidation.

Journal

Account	Amount £	Dr ✓	Cr ✓

(b) A payment of £880 for repairs to the company van has been made from the bank. The correct entry was made to the bank account but no other entries were made.

Journal

Account	Amount £	Dr ✓	Cr ✓

(c) No entries have been made for closing stock for the year end 31 December 20X1. Closing stock has been valued at cost at £31,610.

Journal

Account	Amount £	Dr ✓	Cr ✓

(d) The figures from the columns of the purchases day book for 23 December have been totalled correctly as follows:

Purchases column	£25,000
VAT column	£5,000
Total column	£30,000

The amounts have been posted as follows:

Dr Purchases	£25,000
Cr VAT	£5,000
Cr Purchases ledger control account	£30,000

Journal

Account	Amount £	Dr ✓	Cr ✓

36 JACKSONS

You are working on the final accounts of Jacksons, a business with a year end of 31 May. A trial balance has been drawn up and a suspense account opened with a credit balance of £1,200. You need to make some corrections and adjustments for the year ended 31 May 20X1.

Record the adjustments needed on the extract from the extended trial balance to deal with the items below. (You will not need to enter adjustments on every line)

(i) Entries need to be made for a bad debt of £220.

(ii) A loan repayment of £1,600 has been made. The correct entry was made to the loan account but no other entries were made.

(iii) No entries have been made for closing stock for the year-end 31 May 20X1. Closing stock has been valued at cost at £17,700.

(iv) The figures from the columns of the sales day book for 23 May have been totalled correctly as follows:

Sales column	£2,000
VAT column	£400
Total column	£2,400

The amounts have been posted as follows:

Cr Sales	£2,000
Cr VAT	£400
Dr Sales ledger control account	£2,000

Extract from extended trial balance

	Ledger balances		Adjustments	
	Dr	Cr	Dr	Cr
	£	£	£	£
Accruals		365		
Bank	4,300			
Closing stock – balance sheet				
Closing stock – P&L account				
Depreciation charge				
Bad debts				
Loan		4,000		
Loan interest	240			
Plant and machinery – accumulated		22,000		
Revenue		210,000		
Sales ledger control account	24,500			
Suspense		1,200		
VAT		5,600		

37 HERMES DELIVERIES

Hermes Deliveries has a year end of 31 May. A trial balance has been drawn up and a suspense account opened with a credit balance of £12,525. You need to make some corrections and adjustments for the year ended 31 May 20X1.

Record the journal entries needed in the general ledger to deal with the items below. You do not need to give narrative.

You should remove any incorrect entries, where appropriate, and post the correct entries.

(a) A payment of £275 for printer cartridges and paper has been made from the bank. The correct entry was made to the bank, but no other entries were made.

Journal

Account	Amount £	Dr ✓	Cr ✓

(b) No entries have been made for closing stock, which has been valued at £34,962.

Journal

Account	Amount £	Dr ✓	Cr ✓

(c) Notice has been received of the liquidation of Kat Ltd. The sales ledger account shows a balance of £210 for this customer.

Journal

Account	Amount £	Dr ✓	Cr ✓

(d) The figures from the columns of the sales day book for 15 April have been totalled correctly as follows:

Sales column	£32,000
VAT column	£6,400
Total column	£38,400

The amounts have been posted as follows:

Dr Sales ledger control account	£38,400
Dr VAT	£6,400
Cr Revenue	£32,000

Journal

Account	Amount £	Dr ✓	Cr ✓

38 EVANS AND CO

You are employed by Evans and Co, a bicycle manufacturer as their bookkeeper and they have asked you to create a trial balance. Below are the balances extracted from the main ledger at 31 May 20X0.

(a) Enter the balances into the columns of the trial balance provided below. Total the two columns and enter an appropriate suspense account balance to ensure that the two totals agree.

	£	Debit	Credit
Capital	50,000		
Purchases	83,468		
Revenue	159,407		
Purchase Returns	2,693		
Sales Returns	3,090		
SLCA	25,642		
PLCA	31,007		
Drawings	25,500		
Machinery – Cost	45,900		
Machinery – Accumulated Depreciation	15,925		
Rent and Rates	15,600		
Light and Heat	2,466		
Motor Expenses	2,603		
Loan	12,500		
Interest paid	1,250		
Discounts received	400		
Bad debts	1,300		
Accruals	2,572		
Salaries	77,921		
Bank overdraft	3,876		
Suspense			
Totals			

(b) You are told of the following errors:

(i) Drawings of £1,000 have been debited to the salaries account

(ii) The net column of the PDB has been overcast by £280

(iii) The VAT column of the SDB has been undercast by £70

(iv) An amount of £3,175 paid for rent and rates has been debited to both the rent and rates account and the bank account.

(v) An accrual for electricity at the year end of £340 has been correctly credited to the accruals account but no other entry has been made.

Prepare the entries to correct these errors using the blank journal below. Dates and narratives are not required.

		Amount £	Dr ✓	Cr ✓
(i)				
(ii)				
(iii)				
(iv)				
(v)				

LEVEL II: CERTIFICATE IN MANUAL BOOKKEEPING

39 RACHEL EDMUNDSON

You are employed by Rachel Edmundson who is a florist. You are her bookkeeper and she has asked you to create a trial balance. Below are the balances extracted from the main ledger at 30 April 20X2.

(a) Enter the balances into the columns of the trial balance provided below. Total the two columns and enter an appropriate suspense account balance to ensure that the two totals agree.

	£	Debit	Credit
Accruals	4,820		
Prepayments	2,945		
Motor Expenses	572		
Admin Expenses	481		
Light and Heat	1,073		
Revenue	48,729		
Purchases	26,209		
SLCA	5,407		
PLCA	3,090		
Rent	45		
Purchase Returns	306		
Discounts allowed	567		
Capital	10,000		
Loan	15,000		
Interest paid	750		
Drawings	4,770		
Motor Vehicles – cost	19,000		
Motor Vehicle – accumulated depreciation	2,043		
VAT control (due to HMRC)	2,995		
Wages	20,000		
Suspense Account			
Totals			

(b) Since the trial balance has been produced you have noticed a number of errors which are as follows:

(i) Rachel put £5,000 into the business after receiving a large cheque as a Christmas present from her Gran. This has been put through the bank account but no other entries have been made.

(ii) The Gross column of the SDB has been overcast by £385.

(iii) The VAT column of the PDB has been undercast by £193.

(iv) An amount of £4,500 paid for rent has been credited to both the rent account and the bank account.

(v) An accrual for electricity at the year-end of £1,356 has been correctly credited to the accruals account but no other entry has been made.

Prepare the entries to correct these errors using the blank journal below. Dates and narratives are not required.

		Dr £	Cr £
(i)			
(ii)			
(iii)			
(iv)			
(v)			

DEPRECIATION OF FIXED ASSETS

40 SOUTHGATE TRADING

The following is a purchase invoice received by Southgate Trading, who is registered for VAT:

To: Southgate Trading Unit 26, Three Cliffs Trading Estate Gowerton GW14 6PW	Invoice 535 Computer Supplies plc 12 Hanger Lane Bedgrove	Date: 28 March X9	
			£
HP colour laser printer	Serial number 65438LKR	1	750.00
Delivery		1	25.00
Printer cartridges @ £20.00 each		2	40.00
VAT @ 20%			163.00
Total			978.00
Settlement terms: strictly 30 days net.			

- Southgate Trading has a policy of capitalising expenditure over £500.
- Vehicles are depreciated at 25% on a reducing balance basis.
- Computer equipment is depreciated at 30% on a straight-line basis assuming no residual value.
- Assets are depreciated in the year of acquisition but not in the year of disposal.

Required:

Record the following information in the fixed assets register below:

(a) Any acquisitions of fixed assets during the year ended 31 March X9

(b) Depreciation for the year ended 31 March X9

Fixed assets register

Description	Acquisition date	Cost	Depreciation	Net book value
		£	£	£
Computer equipment				
Server main office	30/09/X6	2,800.00		
Year end 31/03/X7			840.00	1,960.00
Year end 31/03/X8			840.00	1,120.00
Year end 31/03/X9				
Motor vehicles				
AB08 DRF	01/04/X6	12,000.00		
Year end 31/03/X7			3,000.00	9,000.00
Year end 31/03/X8			2,250.00	6,750.00
Year end 31/03/X9				
AB 07 FRP	31/01/X8	9,600.00		
Year end 31/03/X8			2,400.00	7,200.00
Year end 31/03/X9				

41 NON-CURRENT ASSET LEDGERS

- You are working on the accounts of a partnership that is registered for VAT.
- A new vehicle has been acquired. VAT can be reclaimed on this vehicle.
- The cost excluding VAT was £7,500; this was paid from the bank.
- The residual value is expected to be £1,500 excluding VAT.
- The depreciation policy for vehicles is 25% per annum on a straight line basis.
- Depreciation has already been entered into the accounts for the existing vehicles.

Make entries to account for:

(a) The purchase of the new vehicle.

(b) The depreciation on the new vehicle.

On each account, show clearly the balance carried down or transferred to the profit and loss account.

Vehicles at cost

Balance b/d	10,000		

Vehicles accumulated depreciation

		Balance b/d	3,000

Depreciation charge

Balance b/d	1,000		

42 KATY'S CAKES

- Katy's Cakes is a sole trader business that is registered for VAT. Her year end is 30/04/X0.

- A new industrial sized cake mixer has been acquired. VAT can be reclaimed on this piece of equipment.

- The asset was purchased for cash and cost £8,500 (excluding VAT). This was paid from the bank.

- The depreciation policy for equipment is 10% per annum on a reducing balance basis.

- Depreciation on existing equipment has not been accounted for in the year-ended 30/04/X0, however there is some depreciation from other categories of asset and this has already been reflected in the depreciation charge account.

Make entries into the proformas below to account for:

(a) The purchase of the new equipment

(b) The depreciation on the existing assets

(c) The depreciation on the new equipment

On each account, show clearly the balance carried down or transferred to the income statement.

Equipment at cost

Balance b/d	6,200		

Equipment accumulated depreciation

		Balance b/d	1,900

Depreciation charge

Balance b/d	3,000		

(d) Which of the following best describes capital expenditure?

	✓
The money put in by the owners of the business	
The money spent on the purchase of fixed assets	
The total amount of capital owed to the owner of the business	

43 MEAD

Mead is a sole trader with a 31 December year end. He purchased a car on 1 January 20X3 at a cost of £12,000. He estimates that its useful life is four years, after which he will trade it in for £2,400. The annual depreciation charge is to be calculated using the straight line method.

Required:

Write up the motor car cost, accumulated depreciation and depreciation expense accounts for the first three years, bringing down a balance on each account at the end of each year.

44   S TELFORD

S Telford purchases a machine for £6,000. He estimates that the machine will last eight years and its scrap value then will be £1,000.

Required:

(a) Prepare the machine cost and accumulated depreciation accounts for the first three years of the machine's life, and show the balance sheet extract at the end of each of these years charging depreciation on the straight line method.

(b) What would be the net book value of the machine at the end of the third year if depreciation was charged at 20% on the reducing balance method?

45   HILTON

(a) Hillton started a veggie food manufacturing business on 1 January 20X6. During the first three years of trading he bought machinery as follows:

January	20X6	Chopper	Cost	£4,000
April	20X7	Mincer	Cost	£6,000
June	20X8	Stuffer	Cost	£8,000

Each machine was bought for cash.

Hillton's policy for machinery is to charge depreciation on the straight line basis at 25% per annum. A full year's depreciation is charged in the year of purchase, irrespective of the actual date of purchase.

Required

For the three years from 1 January 20X6 to 31 December 20X8 prepare the following ledger accounts:

(i) Machinery account

(ii) Accumulated depreciation account (machinery)

(iii) Depreciation expense account (machinery)

Bring down the balance on each account at 31 December each year.

(b) Over the same three year period Hillton bought the following motor vehicles for his business:

January	20X6	Metro van	Cost	£3,200
July	20X7	Transit van	Cost	£6,000
October	20X8	Astra van	Cost	£4,200

Each vehicle was bought for cash.

Hillton's policy for motor vehicles is to charge depreciation on the reducing balance basis at 40% per annum. A full year's depreciation is charged in the year of purchase, irrespective of the actual date of purchase.

Required

For the three years from 1 January 20X6 to 31 December 20X8 prepare the following ledger accounts:

(i) Motor vehicles account

(ii) Accumulated depreciation account (motor vehicles)

(iii) Depreciation expense account (motor vehicles)

Bring down the balance on each account at 31 December each year.

46 INFORTEC COMPUTERS

On 1 December 20X2 Infortec Computers owned motor vehicles costing £28,400. During the year ended 30 November 20X3 the following changes to the motor vehicles took place:

		£
1 March 20X3	Sold vehicle – original cost	18,000
1 June 20X3	Purchased new vehicle – cost	10,000
1 September 20X3	Purchased new vehicle – cost	12,000

Depreciation on motor vehicles is calculated on a monthly basis at 20% per annum on cost.

Complete the table below to calculate the total depreciation charge to profits for the year ended 30 November 20X3.

	£
Depreciation for vehicle sold 1 March 20X3	....
Depreciation for vehicle purchased 1 June 20X3	....
Depreciation for vehicle purchased 1 September 20X3	....
Depreciation for other vehicles owned during the year	....
Total depreciation for the year ended 30 November 20X3	....

LEVEL II: CERTIFICATE IN MANUAL BOOKKEEPING

ACCRUALS AND PREPAYMENTS

47 ACCRUALS AND PREPAYMENTS (1)

You are given the following information (ignore VAT):

Balances as at:	1 April 20X0
	£
Accrual for administration expenses	790
Prepayment for selling expenses	475

The bank summary for the year shows payments for administration expenses of £7,190. Included in this figure is £2,700 for the quarter ended 31 May 20X1.

(a) **Prepare the administration expenses account for the year ended 31 March 20X1 and close it off by showing the transfer to the income statement**

Administration expenses

(b) The bank summary for the year shows payments for selling expenses of £7,900. In April 20X1, £900 was paid for selling expenses incurred in March 20X1.

Prepare the selling expenses account for the year ended 31 March 20X1 and close it off by showing the transfer to the income statement.

Selling expenses

(c) You have the following extract of balances from the general ledger.

Using your answers to (a) and (b), and the figures given below, enter amounts in the appropriate column for the accounts shown.

Extract from trial balance as at 31 March 20X1

Account	£	Dr £	Cr £
Accruals			
Capital	6,000		
Wages & Salaries	850		
Selling expenses			
Drawings	11,000		
Administration expenses			
Interest received	70		
Machinery at cost	5,600		
Machinery accumulated depreciation	4,200		
Prepayments			

48 ACCRUALS AND PREPAYMENTS (2)

You are given the following information (ignore VAT):

Balances as at:	1 April 20X5 £
Accrual for electricity expenses	2,815
Prepayment for rental expenses	6,250

The bank summary for the year shows payments for electricity expenses of £10,539. Included in this figure is £2,358 for the quarter ended 31 May 20X6.

(a) **Prepare the electricity expenses account for the year ended 31 March 20X6 and close it off by showing the transfer to the income statement.**

Electricity expenses

The bank summary for the year shows payments for rental expenses of £62,500. In April 20X6, £6,250 was paid late relating to March 20X6 rent.

(b) **Prepare the rental expenses account for the year ended 31 March 20X6 and close it off by showing the transfer to the income statement.**

Rental expenses

You have the following extract of balances from the general ledger.

(c) **Using your answers to (a) and (b), and the figures given below, enter amounts in the appropriate column for the accounts shown.**

Extract from trial balance as at 31 March 20X6.

Account	£	Dr £	Cr £
Accruals			
Accumulated depreciation – Office Equipment	17,921		
Depreciation charge	3,805		
Drawings	22,400		
Electricity			
Interest received	129		
Office Equipment – cost	42,784		
Rental			
Stationery	2,800		
Prepayments			

49 SIOBHAN

Siobhan, the proprietor of a sweet shop, provides you with the following information in respect of sundry expenditure and income of her business for the year ended 31 December 20X4:

1 Rent payable

£15,000 was paid during 20X4 to cover the 15 months ending 31 March 20X5.

2 Gas

£840 was paid during 20X4 to cover gas charges from 1 January 20X4 to 31 July 20X4. Gas charges can be assumed to accrue evenly over the year. There was no outstanding balance at 1 January 20X4.

3 Advertising

Included in the payments totalling £3,850 made during 20X4 is an amount of £500 payable in respect of a planned campaign for 20X5.

PRACTICE QUESTIONS: SECTION 1

4 Bank interest

The bank statements of the business show that the following interest has been charged to the account.

For period up to 31 May 20X4	Nil (no overdraft)
For 1 June – 31 August 20X4	£28
1 September – 30 November 20X4	£45

The bank statements for 20X5 show that £69 was charged to the account on 28 February 20X5.

5 Rates

Towards the end of 20X3 £4,800 was paid to cover the six months ended 31 March 20X4.

In May 20X4 £5,600 was paid to cover the six months ended 30 September 20X4.

In early 20X5 £6,600 was paid for the six months ending 31 March 20X5.

6 Rent receivable

During 20X4, Siobhan received £250 rent from Joe Soap for the use of a lock-up garage attached to the shop, in respect of the six months ended 31 March 20X4.

She increased the rent to £600 pa from 1 April 20X4, and during 20X4 Joe Soap paid her rent for the full year ending 31 March 20X5.

Required:

Write up ledger accounts for each of the above items, showing:

(a) the opening balance at 1 January 20X4, if any.

(b) any cash paid or received.

(c) the closing balance at 31 December 20X4.

(d) the charge or credit for the year to the profit and loss account.

50 A CREW

The following is an extract from the trial balance of A Crew at 31 December 20X1:

	Dr
	£
Stationery	560
Rent	900
Rates	380
Lighting and heating	590
Insurance	260
Wages and salaries	2,970

Stationery which had cost £15 was still in hand at 31 December 20X1.

Rent of £300 for the last three months of 20X1 had not been paid and no entry has been made in the books for it.

£280 of the rates was for the year ended 31 March 20X2. The remaining £100 was for the three months ended 31 March 20X1.

Fuel had been delivered on 18 December 20X1 at a cost of £15 and had been consumed before the end of 20X1. No invoice had been received for the £15 fuel in 20X1 and no entry has been made in the records of the business.

£70 of the insurance paid was in respect of insurance cover for the year 20X2.

Nothing was owing to employees for wages and salaries at the close of 20X1.

Required:

Record the above information in the relevant accounts, showing the transfers to the profit and loss account for the year ended 31 December 20X1.

51 A METRO

A Metro owns a number of antique shops and, in connection with this business, he runs a small fleet of motor vans. He prepares his accounts to 31 December in each year.

On 1 January 20X0 the amount prepaid for motor tax and insurance was £570.

On 1 April 20X0 he paid £420 which represented motor tax on six of the vans for the year ended 31 March 20X1.

On 1 May 20X0 he paid £1,770 insurance for all ten vans for the year ended 30 April 20X1.

On 1 July 20X0 he paid £280 which represented motor tax for the other four vans for the year ended 30 June 20X1.

Required:

Write up the account for 'motor tax and insurance' for the year ended 31 December 20X0.

BAD DEBTS

52 PUTNEY

Putney, a sole trader, has the following balances at the year-ended 31 December 20X8

	£
Debtors at 1.1.X8	34,500
Cash received from credit customers	229,900
Contra with payables	1,200
Discounts allowed	17,890
Cash sales	24,000
Bad debts	18,600
Increase in provisions for doubtful debt	12,500
Discounts received	15,670
Debtors at 31.12.X8	45,000

What is the revenue figure reported by Putney in the year ended 31 December 20X8?

£ [ ]

53 PURDEY

The following account has been extracted from the nominal ledger of Purdey:

Debtors ledger control account

	£		£
Balance b/d	84,700		
Contra with creditors ledger control account	5,000	Bad debts	4,300
Discounts received	21,100	Discounts allowed	30,780
Credit sales	644,000	Cash received from credit customers	595,000
Cash sales	13,500	Increase in provision for bad debt	6,555
		Balance c/d	131,665
	768,300		768,300

Rewrite the debtors ledger control account, correct any errors in the original.

Debtors ledger control account

	£		£
Balance b/d	84,700		
	———		———
	———		———

54 BORIS

In the balance sheet at 31 December 20X5, Boris reported debtors of £12,000. During 20X6 he made sales on credit of £125,000 and received cash from credit customers amounting to £115,500. At 31 December 20X6, Boris wished to write off debts of £7,100. What is the debtors figure at 31 December 20X6?

£	

55 FAUNTLEROY

In the year ended 30 September 20X8, Fauntleroy had sales of £7,000,000, of which £1 million related to cash sales. During the year bad debts amounting to £3,200 were written off and there was a £2,700 contra with the purchase ledger control account. If year-end debtors were £745,000 and £5.36 million has been received from credit customers in the year, what was the balance b/d for opening debtors at the beginning of the year?

£	

56 TIPTON

On 1 January 20X3 Tipton's trade debtors were £10,000. The following relates to the year ended 31 December 20X3:

	£
Credit sales	100,000
Cash receipts	90,000
Discounts allowed	800
Discounts received	700

On 31 December 20X3 debtors were:

£ [   ]

57

Headington is owed £37,500 by its customers at the start, and £39,000 at the end, of its year ended 31 December 20X8.

During the period, cash sales of £263,500 and credit sales of £357,500 were made, discounts allowed amounted to £15,750 and discounts received £21,400. Bad debts of £10,500 were written off.

The cash received from debtors in the year totalled:

A £329,750

B £593,175

C £593,250

D £614,650

FINAL ACCOUNTS OF A SOLE TRADER

58 PG TRADING

You have the following trial balance for a sole trader known as PG Trading. All the necessary year-end adjustments have been made.

PG Trading		
Trial balance as at 30 September 20X8		
	Dr £	Cr £
Accruals		4,100
Bank	3,500	
Capital		10,100
Closing stock	19,500	19,500
Depreciation charge	7,100	
Discounts allowed	1,350	
Drawings	11,000	
General expenses	26,100	
Machinery at cost	26,000	
Machinery accumulated depreciation		15,000
Opening stock	17,700	
Prepayments	4,600	
Purchases	98,000	
Purchases ledger control account		32,000
Rent	7,300	
Sales		170,850
Sales ledger control account	26,400	
VAT		5,500
Wages	8,500	
	257,050	257,050

(a) Prepare a profit and loss account for the business for the year ended 30 September 20X8.

PG Trading		
Profit and loss account for the year ended 30 September 20X8		
	£	£
Sales		
Cost of goods sold		
Gross profit		
Less:		
Total expenses		
Net profit for the year		

(b) Indicate where the bank balance (£3,500 debit) should be shown in the financial statements. Choose ONE.

  (i) Fixed assets

  (ii) Current assets

  (iii) Expenses in the income statement

  (iv) Creditors due within one year

59 STOCK TRADING

You have the following trial balance for a sole trader known as Stock Trading. All the necessary year-end adjustments have been made.

Stock Trading

Trial balance as at 30 September 20X9

	Dr £	Cr £
Accruals		1,590
Bank Overdraft		1,250
Capital		15,500
Closing stock	7,850	7,850
Discounts Received		900
Sundry creditors		1,450
Purchase ledger control account		6,800
Depreciation charge	1,600	
Discounts allowed	345	
Bad debts	295	
Drawings	6,500	
Equipment at cost	17,500	
Equipment accumulated depreciation		4,500
Prepayments	3,200	
Sales ledger control account	7,800	
Wages	24,000	
Rent	5,250	
Disposal		450
Sales Returns	1,500	
Opening Stock	3,450	
Purchases	125,000	
General expenses	2,950	
Revenue		164,000
VAT		2,950
	207,240	207,240

(a) Prepare a profit and loss account for the business for the year ended 30 September 20X9.

Stock Trading		
Profit and loss account for the year ended 30 September 20X9		
	£	£
Sales		
Cost of goods sold		
Gross profit		
Add:		
Total Sundry Income		
Less:		
Total expenses		
Net profit for the year		

(b) Indicate where the drawings should be shown in the financial statements. Choose ONE.

    (i) As an addition to capital

    (ii) As a deduction from capital

    (iii) As an addition to expenses

    (iv) As a deduction from expenses

60 TONY BROWN

Tony Brown is a self employed joiner. His trial balance as at 31 March 20X7 was as follows:

	Dr £	Cr £
Capital		30,000
Bank Loan		4,500
Motor Vehicles	17,000	
Tools and Equipment	19,600	
Office Equipment	4,000	
Opening stocks	1,500	
Bank	1,280	
Cash	100	
Debtors	3,600	
Creditors		2,100
VAT Account		800
Sales		80,000
Purchases	34,500	
Repairs and Maintenance	1,520	
Motor Vehicle Running Costs	3,450	
Insurances	1,250	
Office Expenses	600	
Wages	8,000	
Drawings	21,000	
	117,400	117,400

Closing stock at 31 March 20X7 was valued at £1,620.

(a) Prepare a profit and loss account for Tony Brown for the year ended 31 March 20X7.

Profit and loss account for the year ended 31 March 20X7		
	£	£
Sales		
Cost of goods sold		
Gross profit		
Less:		
Total expenses		
Profit for the year		

(b) Prepare a balance sheet for Tony Brown as at 31 March 20X7.

Balance sheet as at 31 March 20X7		
	£	£
Fixed assets		
Current assets		
Creditors due within one year		
Net current assets		
Total assets less current liabilities		
Long term liabilities		
Net assets		
Financed by:		
Capital		
Profit for the year		
Drawings		

61 JOHN RISDON

John Risdon is a self-employed plumber and his trial balance as at 31 March 2007 showed:

	Dr £	Cr £
Capital		36,000
Bank Loan		6,500
Motor Vehicle	18,500	
Tools and Equipment	20,000	
Office Equipment	5,000	
Stock	1,750	
Bank	4,000	
Cash	450	
Debtors	4,100	
Creditors		2,600
VAT Account		1,000
Sales		84,500
Purchase	38,100	
Repairs and Maintenance	1,750	
Insurance	1,400	
Motor Vehicle Running Costs	4,100	
Office Expenses	700	
Wages	8,750	
Drawings	22,000	
	130,600	130,600

Stocks of materials as at 31 March 2007 were £1,850.

Task

Prepare the profit and loss account for year ended 31 March 20X7 together with a balance sheet as that date.

62 ANDREW FEWSTER

Andrew Fewster is a self employed painter and decorator his trial balance as at 31 March 20X7 showed:

	Dr	Cr
Capital		37,500
Bank Loan		10,500
Motor Vehicle	22,500	
Tools and Equipment	21,000	
Office Equipment	5,500	
Stocks of Materials	1,950	
Bank	1,000	
Cash	200	
Debtors	5,500	
Creditors		2,950
VAT Account		1,400
Sales		86,500
Purchases	39,500	
Repairs and Maintenance	1,950	
Motor Vehicles Running Costs	4,250	
Insurance	1,850	
Office Expenses	950	
Wages	9,200	
Drawings	23,500	
	138,850	138,850

Adjustments required:

- Stocks of materials at 31 March 2007 £2,150.
- Depreciation is to be provided on:
  - Motor Vehicles £5,625
  - Tools and Equipment £5,250
  - Office Equipment £1,375
- Adjustments for insurance prepayments of £250 and office expense accruals of £50 need to be made.

Required:

Prepare the profit and loss account for year ended 31 March 20X7 together with a balance sheet as that date.

Section 2

PRACTICE ANSWERS

ACCOUNTING FOR VAT

1   VAT RELATED TERMS

Output tax:	tax charged on the sale of goods and services. This is collected from customers and paid to HMRC.
Input tax:	tax charged on purchases of goods and services. This is paid to suppliers and then recovered from HMRC.
Zero-rated item:	these are items specifically identified as having a 0% VAT rate. Companies that sell zero rated items can still reclaim VAT on purchases.
Exempt item:	these are items that have been specifically identified as having no VAT. If a business sells VAT exempt items it cannot reclaim VAT on purchases.
Standard rated:	these include all other items that are charged at a standard rate, which is fixed for a period of time by the relevant Finance Act. The standard rate is currently 20%.
Tax point:	this is the date a transaction takes place for VAT purposes. This typically refers to the date that goods and services are supplied to the customer, although there are exceptions to this principle.

2   ERIN

(a)

	£
Price	600
Less: trade discount (5% × £600)	(30)
	570
Less: Cash/settlement discount (3% × £570)	(17.10)
Amount chargeable to VAT	552.90
VAT at 20% × £552.90	**110.58**

(b) If Kyle fails to take the prompt payment discount he will pay the sale price (less the trade discount) plus VAT:

£570.00 + £110.58 =

£680.58

KAPLAN PUBLISHING

3 LAUREL

VAT Control Account

	£		£
		Balance b/d	23,778
Tax on purchases	100,560	Tax on sales	160,000
Balance c/d	83,218		
	183,778		183,778
		Balance b/d	83,218

VAT on sales: £800,000 × 20% = £160,000

VAT on purchases: £603,360 × 20/120 = £100,560

4 SALES AND PURCHASES

(a)

VAT Control Account

	£		£
Tax on purchases		Tax on sales	4,602.08
(£18,000 × 20%)	3,600.00	(£27,612.5 × 20/120)	
Balance c/d	1,002.08		
	4,602.08		4,602.08
		Balance b/d	**1,002.08**

(b) The balance b/d is a creditor, therefore this represents amounts due **to** HMRC.

5 RAMSGATE

VAT Control Account

	£		£
Tax on purchases	6,714.33	Balance b/d	3,400.00
Bank	2,600.00	Tax on sales	12,000.00
Balance c/d	6,085.67		
	15,400.00		15,400.00
		Balance b/d	6,085.67

Tax on sales (outputs) = 20% × £60,000 = £12,000

Tax on purchases (inputs) = (20/120) × £40,286 = £6,714.33

6 LAKER

Account name	Amount £	Debit ✓	Credit ✓
Purchase ledger control account	240	✓	
VAT control account	40		✓
Purchase returns	200		✓

7 A

- If input tax (tax on purchases) exceeds output tax (tax on sales), the difference is recoverable from the tax authorities.
- Sales and purchases are reported net of VAT.
- VAT cannot be recovered on certain expenses (such as client entertaining) and purchases (such as cars).

8 DUNCAN BYE

Value Added Tax Return

For the period

01/04/X1 to 30/06/X1

HM Customs and Excise

Duncan Bye
Low House
Low Green
Derbyshire
DE1 7XU

140784/06

Your VAT Office telephone number is 0151 644211

For Official Use

Registration number: 131 7250 19

Period: 06 X1

You could be liable to a financial penalty if your completed return and all the VAT payable are not received by the due date.

Due date: 31.07.X1

If you may trade or pay taxes in euro from Jan 1999. Contact your Business Advice Centre for C&E queries or Treasury Enquiry Unit on 0171 270 4558

Before you fill in this form read the notes on the back and the VAT leaflet *'Filling in your VAT Return'*. Fill in all boxes clearly in ink, and write 'none' where necessary. Don't put a dash or leave any box blank. If there are no pence write '00' in the pence column. **Do not** enter more than one amount in any box.

		£	p
VAT due in this period on **sales** and other outputs		4,324	00
VAT due in this period on **acquisitions** from other **EC Member States**		None	
Total VAT due (**the sum of boxes 1 and 2**)		4,324	00
VAT reclaimed in this period on **purchases** and other inputs (including acquisitions from the EC)		1,835	12
		2,488	88
Total value of **sales** and all other outputs excluding any VAT. **Include your box 8 figure.**		21,620	00
Total value of **purchases** and all other inputs excluding any VAT. **Include your box 9 figure.**		9,176	00
Total value of all **supplies** of goods and related services, excl any VAT, to other **EC Member States.**		None	00
Total value of all **acquisitions** of goods and related servs, excl any VAT, from other **EC Member States.**		None	00

Retail schemes. If you have used any of the schemes in the period covered by this return, enter the relevant letter(s) in this box.

If you are enclosing a payment please tick this box.

DECLARATION: You, or someone on your behalf, must sign below.

I, ...DUNCAN BYE.. declare that the
(Full name of signatory in BLOCK LETTERS)
information given above is true and complete.
Signature.. Date .... 19..........
A false declaration can result in prosecution.

0141846

VAT 100 (Full)   PCU (June 1996)   F

Workings:

VAT on sales:

	£
VAT on sales	4,300.00
VAT on personal goods used (£120.00 × 20%)	24.00
	4,324.00

VAT on purchases:

	£
VAT on purchases	1,820.00
VAT on petty cash expenditure	15.12
	1,835.12

9 MARK AMBROSE

Value Added Tax Return

For the period 01/07/X1 to 30/09/X1

For Official Use

Registration number: 123 9872 17

Period: 09 X1

HM Customs and Excise

Mark Ambrose
High Park House
High Melton

Your VAT Office telephone number is 0151 644211

You could be liable to a financial penalty if your completed return and all the VAT payable are not received by the due date.

Due date: 31.10.X1

ATTENTION

If you may trade or pay taxes in euro from Jan 1999, Contact your Business Advice Centre for C&E queries or Treasury Enquiry Unit on 020 7270 4558

Before you fill in this form read the notes on the back and the VAT leaflet *'Filling in your VAT Return'*. Fill in all boxes clearly in ink, and write 'none' where necessary. Don't put a dash or leave any box blank. If there are no pence write '00' in the pence column. **Do not** enter more than one amount in any box.

		£	p
VAT due in this period on **sales** and other outputs	1	7,780	00
VAT due in this period on **acquisitions** from other **EC Member States**	2	None	
Total VAT due (**the sum of boxes 1 and 2**)	3	7,780	00
VAT reclaimed in this period on **purchases** and other inputs (including acquisitions from the EC)	4	3,428	00
Net VAT to be paid to Customs or reclaimed by you (Difference between boxes 3 and 4)	5	4,352	00
Total value of **sales** and all other outputs excluding any VAT. **Include your box 8 figure.**	6	38,900	00
Total value of **purchases** and all other inputs excluding any VAT. **Include your box 9 figure.**	7	16,740	00
Total value of all **supplies** of goods and related services, excl any VAT, to other **EC Member States.**	8	None	00
Total value of all **acquisitions** of goods and related servs, excl any VAT, from other **EC Member States.**	9	None	00

Retail schemes. If you have used any of the schemes in the period covered by this return, enter the relevant letter(s) in this box.

If you are enclosing a payment please tick this box.

DECLARATION: You, or someone on your behalf, must sign below.

I, ... MARK AMBROSE .... declare that the
(Full name of signatory in BLOCK LETTERS)
information given above is true and complete.
Signature.................................... Date .... 20............

VAT 100 (Full)   0141846   PCU (June 1996)   F

Workings:

VAT on sales:

	£
VAT on sales	7,680.00
VAT on personal goods used (£500.00 × 20%)	100.00
	7,780.00

VAT on purchases:

The VAT reclaimed includes relief on bad debts that are over six months old at the date of return. Total VAT reclaimed is therefore calculated as follows:

	£
VAT on purchases	3,294.00
VAT on petty cash purchases (£324.00 × 20/120)	54.00
VAT on bad debts ((£300 + £180) × 20/120)	80.00
	3,428.00

LEVEL II: CERTIFICATE IN MANUAL BOOKKEEPING

10 SIMON WHITE ACCOUNTANCY

Value Added Tax Return

For the period

01/07/X1 to 30/09/X1

HM Customs and Excise

John Thistle
t/as Crescent Hotel
High Street
Whitby
YO21 37L   140784/06

Your VAT Office telephone number is 0151 644211

For Official Use

Registration number: 179 6421 27

Period: 09 X1

You could be liable to a financial penalty if your completed return and all the VAT payable are not received by the due date.

Due date: 31.10.X1

ATTENTION

If you may trade or pay taxes in euro from Jan 1999, Contact your Business Advice Centre for C&E queries or Treasury Enquiry Unit on 020 7270 4558

Before you fill in this form read the notes on the back and the VAT leaflet *'Filling in your VAT Return'*. Fill in all boxes clearly in ink, and write 'none' where necessary. Don't put a dash or leave any box blank. If there are no pence write '00' in the pence column. **Do not** enter more than one amount in any box.

			£	p
For official use	VAT due in this period on **sales** and other outputs	1	16,520	00
	VAT due in this period on **acquisitions** from other **EC Member States**	2	None	
	Total VAT due (**the sum of boxes 1 and 2**)	3	16,520	00
	VAT reclaimed in this period on **purchases** and other inputs (including acquisitions from the EC)	4	5,646	29
	Net VAT to be paid to Customs or reclaimed by you (Difference between boxes 3 and 4)	5	7,006	71
	Total value of **sales** and all other outputs excluding any VAT. **Include your box 8 figure.**	6	82,600	00
	Total value of **purchases** and all other inputs excluding any VAT. **Include your box 9 figure.**	7	27,731	45
	Total value of all **supplies** of goods and related services, excl any VAT, to other **EC Member States**.	8	None	00
	Total value of all **acquisitions** of goods and related servs. excl any VAT, from other **EC Member States**.	9	None	00

Retail schemes. If you have used any of the schemes in the period covered by this return, enter the relevant letter(s) in this box.

If you are enclosing a payment please tick this box.

DECLARATION: You, or someone on your behalf, must sign below.
I, ...JOHN THISTLE.. declare that the
(Full name of signatory in BLOCK LETTERS)
information given above is true and complete.
Signature.. Date .... 20............
A false declaration can result in prosecution.

VAT 100 (Full)   0141846
PCU (June 1996)   F

Workings:

VAT on sales:

	£
VAT on sales	11,020.00
VAT on cash takings (£32,640 x 20/120)	5,440.00
VAT on personal goods used (£300.00 x 20%)	60.00
	16,520.00

VAT on purchases:

The VAT reclaimed includes relief on bad debts that are over six months old at the date of return. Total VAT reclaimed is therefore calculated as follows:

	£
VAT on purchases	3,306.00
VAT from bar and restaurant	2,160.00
VAT on petty cash purchases (£481.75 x 20/120)	80.29
VAT on bad debts (£600 x 20/120)	100.00
	5,646.29

THE CASH BOOK AND THE PETTY CASH BOOK

11 HICKORY HOUSE

Account name	Amount £	Debit ✓	Credit ✓
Cash in hand	34.20	✓	
Postage	15.00	✓	
Motor expenses	12.40	✓	
Office expenses	21.60	✓	
VAT control account	6.80		✓
Bank	90		

12 MESSI & CO

Account name	Amount £	Debit ✓	Credit ✓
VAT	7.25	✓	
Postage	4.50	✓	
Motor Expenses	8.00	✓	
Office Expenses	28.28	✓	
Cash in hand	48.03		✓

13 PETTY CASH

(a) **Petty cash vouchers**

Petty cash voucher	
Date:	7.07.XX
Number:	PC256
Envelopes	
Net	**£14.00**
VAT	**£2.80**
Gross	**£16.80**

Petty cash voucher	
Date:	7.07.XX
Number:	PC257
Motor Fuel	
Net	**£20.00**
VAT	**£4.00**
Gross	**£24.00**

(b) **Reconciliation**

Amount in petty cash box	£141.00
Balance on petty cash account	£145.00
Difference	£4.00

(c) **Imprest restoration**

Petty cash reimbursement	
Date: 31.07.20XX	
Amount required to restore the cash in the petty cash box.	£122.75

14 THE ARCHES

Debit side		Credit side					
Details	Amount £	Details	Amount £	VAT £	Postage £	Travel £	Stationery £
Balance b/d	200.00	Mick's Motors	20.00			20.00	
		Stamps	19.00		19.00		
		Office Essentials	26.40	4.40			22.00
		Balance c/d	134.60				
	200.00		200.00	4.40	19.00	20.00	22.00

15 PETTY CASH VOUCHERS

Petty cash book										
Receipts			Payments							
Date	Detail	Total	Date	Detail	Voucher no	Total	Postage	Staff welfare	Stationery	Travel	VAT
		£				£	£	£	£	£	£
5/1/X1	Bal b/d	150.00	12/1/X1	Postage	03526	13.68	13.68				
				Staff welfare	03527	25.00		25.00			
				Stationery	03528	14.80			12.34		2.46
				Taxi fare	03529	12.00				10.00	2.00
				Staff welfare	03530	6.40		6.40			
				Postage	03531	12.57	12.57				
				Rail fare	03532	6.80				6.80	
				Stationery	03533	7.99			6.66		1.33
				Taxi fare	03534	18.80				15.67	3.13
						118.04	26.25	31.40	19.00	32.47	8.92

CHEQUE REQUISITION FORM

CHEQUE DETAILS

Date   12/1/X1

Payee   Cash

Amount £   118.04

Reason   To restore petty cash

Invoice no (attached/to follow)   –

Receipt (attached/to follow)   –

Required by   (Print)   PETTY CASHIER

              (Signature)   Petty Cashier

Authorised by: ....

Main ledger accounts

Postage account

		£		£
5 Jan	Balance b/d	248.68		
12 Jan	PCB	26.25		

Staff welfare account

		£		£
5 Jan	Balance b/d	225.47		
12 Jan	PCB	31.40		

Stationery account

		£		£
5 Jan	Balance b/d	176.57		
12 Jan	PCB	19.00		

Travel expenses account

		£		£
5 Jan	Balance b/d	160.90		
12 Jan	PCB	32.47		

VAT account

		£			£
12 Jan	PCB	8.92	5 Jan	Balance b/d	2,385.78

PRACTICE ANSWERS: SECTION 2

16 IMPREST SYSTEM

Voucher total

	£
02634	13.73
02635	8.91
02636	10.57
02637	3.21
02638	11.30
02639	14.66
	62.38

Cash total

		£
£10 note	1	10.00
£5 note	2	10.00
£2 coin	3	6.00
£1 coin	7	7.00
50p coin	5	2.50
20p coin	4	0.80
10p coin	1	0.10
5p coin	2	0.10
2p coin	3	0.06
1p coin	6	0.06
		36.62

Reconciliation of cash and vouchers at 22 May 20X1

	£
Voucher total	62.38
Cash total	36.62
	99.00

The reconciliation shows that there is £1 missing. More cash has been paid out of the petty cash box than is supported by the petty cash vouchers. This could be due to a number of reasons:

- A petty cash claim was made out for, say, £11.30 but mistakenly the amount given to the employee was £12.30.

- An employee borrowed £1 from the petty cash box for business expenses and this has not been recorded on a petty cash voucher.

- £1 has been stolen from the petty cash box.

17 IMPREST SYSTEM (2)

Claimed by	Amount	Comment
J Athersych	£7.04	Valid
J Athersych	£4.85	Valid – less than £5
F Rivers	£12.80	Valid – authorised by department head
M Patterson	£6.60	Cannot be paid – no receipt
D R Ray	£42.80	Cannot be paid – more than £30
J Athersych	£3.70	Valid – less than £5
D R Ray	£12.50	Cannot be paid – not authorised by department head
M Patterson	£19.50	Valid
M T Noble	£17.46	Valid
J Norman	£7.60	Cannot be paid – not authorised by department head

18 IMPREST SYSTEM (3)

Petty cash book											
Receipts			Payments								
Date	Detail	Total	Date	Detail	Voucher no	Total	Postage	Stationery	Tea & coffee	Travel	VAT
		£				£	£	£	£	£	£
	Bal b/d	100.00	30/4/X1	Coffee/milk	2534	4.68			4.68		
				Postage	2535	13.26	13.26				
				Stationery	2536	10.27		8.56			1.71
				Taxi fare	2537	15.00				12.50	2.50
				Postage	2538	6.75	6.75				
				Train fare	2539	7.40				7.40	
				Stationery	2540	3.86		3.22			0.64
						61.22	20.01	11.78	4.68	19.90	4.85

Main ledger accounts

Postage account

		£		£
23 Apr	Balance b/d	231.67		
30 Apr	PCB	20.01		

Stationery account

		£		£
23 Apr	Balance b/d	334.78		
30 Apr	PCB	11.78		

Tea and coffee account

		£		£
23 Apr	Balance b/d	55.36		
30 Apr	PCB	4.68		

Travel expenses account

		£		£
23 Apr	Balance b/d	579.03		
30 Apr	PCB	19.90		

VAT account

		£			£
30 Apr	PCB	4.85	23 Apr	Balance b/d	967.44

BANK RECONCILIATION STATEMENTS

19   RIVERS LTD

Date 20XX	Details	Bank £	Date 20XX	Cheque number	Details	Bank £
01 June	Balance b/d	3,115	01 June	111013	Indigo Beds	650
17 June	Bracken Ltd	300	01 June	111014	DirectFit	1,420
21 June	Airfleet Interiors	560	01 June	111015	Langdon	60
22 June	Harris Homes	333	01 June	111016	QPF Ltd	615
12 June	Ayreshire Build	970	02 June	111017	OMD Ltd	815
23 June	Bank Interest	15	02 June	111018	Hamden Ltd	450
			13 June	111019	Freeman and Cope	522
			13 June		COLLINS	175
			20 June		Rent	500
			23 June		Bank charges	20
			23 June		Balance c/d	66
		5,293				5,293
24 June	Balance b/d	66				

Balance per bank statement	£510
Add:	
Name: Airfleet Interiors	£560
Name: Harris Homes	£333
Total to add	£893
Less:	
Name: OMD Ltd	£815
Name: Freeman and Cope	£522
Total to subtract	£1,337
Balance as per cash book	£66

20 LUXURY BATHROOMS

Date	Details	Bank £	Date	Cheque	Details	Bank £
01 April	Balance b/f	17,845	01 April	120045	R Sterling Ltd	8,850
19 April	Olsen & Lane	2,150	01 April	120046	Bert Cooper	2,250
22 April	Frith Ltd	685	01 April	120047	Hetko & Sons	64
22 April	Hodgetts & Co	282	02 April	120048	Barrett Ltd	3,256
04 April	Ricketts & Co	465	02 April	120049	K Plomer	542
			08 April	120050	I&E Brown	655
			08 April	120051	T Roberts	1,698
			14 April		AMB Ltd	2,265
			14 April		D Draper	2,950
			22 April		Bank charges	63
			23 April		Overdraft fee	25
24 April	Balance c/d	1,191				
		22,618				22,618
			25 April		Balance b/d	1,191

Balance per bank statement	£82
Add:	
Name: Frith Ltd	£685
Name: Hodgetts & Co	£282
Total to add	£967
Less:	
Name: K Plomer	£542
Name: T Roberts	£1,698
Total to subtract	£2,240
Balance as per cash book	£1,191 (overdraft)

21 BANK RECONCILIATION (1)

Adjustment	Amount £	Debit/Credit
Adjustment for (1)	82	Cr
Adjustment for (2)	90	Dr
Adjustment for (4)	1,750	Dr

Cash book (for illustration)

Balance b/d	5,472	Adjustment (1)	82
Adjustment (2)	90		
Adjustment (4)	1,750		
		Balance c/d	7,230
	7,312		7,312

22 BANK RECONCILIATION (2)

Balance on the cash book

	£
Opening balance	860.40
Add: receipts	6,151.01
Less: payments	(4,046.73)
Closing balance	2,964.68

The amended closing balance on the cash book is £2,964.68 whilst the balance shown on the bank statement is £2,293.54. The difference is due to:

- paying in slips 0065 and 0066 have not yet cleared the banking system;

- cheque numbers 012382, 012385, 012388, 012389 and 012390 have not yet cleared the banking system.

Cash receipts book

Date	Narrative	Total £	VAT £	Debtors £	Other £	Discount £
20X1						
7/3	Paying in slip 0062	1,147.45 ✓	90.05	583.52	450.28	23.60
8/3	Paying in slip 0063	1,086.41 ✓	68.84	643.34	344.22	30.01
9/3	Paying in slip 0064	1,332.01 ✓	81.37	809.59	406.85	34.20
10/3	Paying in slip 0065	1,012.95	57.02	652.76	285.14	18.03
11/3	Paying in slip 0066	1,158.46	59.24	779.88	296.22	23.12
	BGC – L Fernley	406.90		406.90		
	Bank interest	6.83			6.83	
		6,151.01	356.52	3,875.99	1,789.54	128.96

Cash payments book

Date	Details	Cheque No	Code	Total £	VAT £	Creditors £	Cash purchases £	Other £	Discount received £
20X1									
7/3	P Barn	012379	PL06	383.21 ✓		383.21			
	Purchases	012380	ML	274.04 ✓	45.67		228.37		
	R Trevor	012381	PL12	496.80 ✓		496.80			6.30
8/3	F Nunn	012382	PL07	218.32		218.32			
	F Taylor	012383	PL09	467.28 ✓		467.28			9.34
	C Cook	012384	PL10	301.40 ✓		301.40			
9/3	L White	012385	PL17	222.61		222.61			
	Purchases	012386	ML	275.13 ✓	45.85		229.28		
	T Finn	012387	PL02	148.60 ✓		148.60			
10/3	S Penn	012388	PL16	489.23		489.23			7.41
11/3	P Price	012389	PL20	299.99		299.99			
	Purchases	012390	ML	270.12	45.02		225.10		
	Loan Finance	SO	ML	200.00				200.00	
				4,046.73	136.54	3,027.44	682.75	200.00	23.05

Bank Statement

FINANCIAL BANK plc CONFIDENTIAL

You can bank on us!

10 Yorkshire Street Account   CURRENT   Sheet 00614
Headingley   Account name T R FABER
Leeds LS1 1QT
Telephone: 0113 633061

Statement date 11 March 20X1   Account Number 27943316

Date	Details	Withdrawals (£)	Deposits (£)	Balance (£)
7/3	Balance from sheet 00613			860.40
	Bank giro credit L Fernley		406.90	1,267.30
9/3	Cheque 012380	268.33 ✓		
	Cheque 012381	496.80 ✓		
	Credit 0062		1,112.60 ✓	1,614.77
10/3	Cheque 012383	467.28 ✓		
	Cheque 012384	301.40 ✓		
	Credit 0063		1,047.80 ✓	
	SO – Loan Finance	200.00		1,693.89
11/3	Cheque 012379	383.21 ✓		
	Cheque 012386	269.40 ✓		
	Cheque 012387	148.60 ✓		
	Credit 0064		1,287.64 ✓	
	Bank interest		6.83	2,187.15

| SO | Standing order | DD | Direct debit | CP | Card purchase |
| AC | Automated cash | OD | Overdrawn | TR | Transfer |

23 BANK RECONCILIATION (3)

Cash book

Receipts		£	Payments		£
16/4	Donald & Co	225.47 ✓	16/4	Balance b/d	310.45
17/4	Harper Ltd	305.68 ✓	17/4	Cheque 03621	204.56
	Fisler Partners	104.67 ✓	18/4	Cheque 03622	150.46 ✓
18/4	Denver Ltd	279.57 ✓	19/4	Cheque 03623	100.80
19/4	Gerald Bros	310.45		Cheque 03624	158.67 ✓
20/4	Johnson & Co	97.68	20/4	Cheque 03625	224.67
			20/4	Balance c/d	173.91
		1,323.52			1,323.52

There are three unticked items on the bank statement:

- Direct debit £183.60 to the District Council

- Cheque number 03621 £240.56 – this has been entered into the cash book as £204.56

- Bank interest £3.64.

There are other unticked items in the cash book but these are payments and receipts that have not yet cleared through the banking system.

EXPRESS BANK

CONFIDENTIAL

You can bank on us!

High Street
Fenbury
TL4 6JY
Telephone: 0169 422130

Account **CURRENT**
Account name **P L DERBY LTD**
Sheet **0213**
Statement date **20 April 20X1**
Account Number **40429107**

Date	Details	Withdrawals (£)	Deposits (£)	Balance (£)
16/4	Balance from sheet 0212			310.45 OD
17/4	DD – District Council	183.60		494.05 OD
18/4	Credit		225.47 ✓	268.58 OD
19/4	Credit		104.67 ✓	
	Cheque 03621	240.56		
	Bank interest	3.64		408.11 OD
20/4	Credit		305.68 ✓	
	Credit		279.57 ✓	
	Cheque 03622	150.46 ✓		
	Cheque 03624	158.67 ✓		131.99 OD

SO	Standing order	DD	Direct debit	CP	Card purchase
AC	Automated cash	OD	Overdrawn	TR	Transfer

24 GRAHAM

(a)

Cash account

	£		£
Balance b/d	204	Sundry accounts	
Interest on deposit account	18	Standing orders	35
		Bank charges	14
		Balance c/d	173
	222		222
Balance b/d	173		

(b) **BANK RECONCILIATION STATEMENT AT 31 MARCH 20X3**

	£
Balance per bank statement	2,618
Add: Uncleared lodgements	723
	3,341
Less: Unpresented cheques	(3,168)
Balance per cash account	173

25 KIVETON CLEANING

BANK RECONCILIATION STATEMENT AS AT 30 JUNE 20X1

	£	£
Balance per bank statement		1,160.25 O/D
Outstanding lodgements:		
30 June		6,910.25
		5,750.00
Unpresented cheques:		
121	538.00	
122	212.00	
		(750.00)
Balance per cash book		£5,000.00

26 NATURAL PRODUCTS LTD

(a) **Cash book receipts**

Date	Narrative	Paying in Slip	Total	Debtors	Mail order	VAT control	Discount allowed
26/6	Trade debtors	598	15,685.23	✓ 15,685.23			
	Mail order (Chq/PO)	599	394.51	✓	328.76	65.75	
	Mail order (CC)	600	91.71		76.43	15.28	
27/6	Trade debtors	601	6,650.28	✓ 6,650.28			
	Mail order	602	118.45	✓	98.71	19.74	
	Megastores plc	CHAPS	11,755.25	✓ 11,755.25			204.17
28/6	Trade debtors	603	12,223.81	✓ 12,223.81			
	Mail order	604	622.18	✓	518.49	103.69	
29/6	Trade debtors	605	5,395.40	5,395.40			
	Mail order	606	100.69		83.91	16.78	
30/6	Trade debtors	607	2,641.68	2,641.68			
	Mail Order/shop	608	254.91		212.43	42.48	
29/6	Freeman Foods	CHAPS	14,776.04	✓ 14,776.04			256.64
30/6	Totals		70,710.14	69,127.69	1,318.73	263.72	460.81

Cash book payments

Date	Narrative	Chq. No	Total	Creditors	Salaries	Other	VAT control	Discount received
26/6	Blackwood Foodstuffs	389	325.99	✓ 325.99				
	Bruning & Soler	390	683.85	✓ 683.85				
	Dehlavi Kosmetatos	391	2,112.16	✓ 2,112.16				
	Environmentally Friendly Co Ltd	392	705.77	705.77				
	Greig Handling (Import)	393	1,253.98	✓ 1,253.98				
	Halpern Freedman	394	338.11	✓ 338.11				
	Kobo Design Studio	395	500.00	✓ 500.00				
	Rayner Food Co	396	375.22	375.22				
	Year 2000 Produce Co	397	1,100.68	1,100.68				
27/6	HM Customs & Excise	398	23,599.28				23,599.28	
28/6	Salaries - Bank Giro	400	48,995.63		48,995.63			
30/6	Arthur Chong Ltd	401	235.55	235.55				
	Dwyer & Co (Import)	402	469.55	469.55				23.48
	Earthworld Ltd	403	449.28	449.28				22.46
	English Electricity	DD	163.17	✓		135.98	27.19	
	English Telecom	DD	229.24	✓		191.04	38.20	
	Totals		81,537.46	8,550.14	48,995.63	327.02	23,664.67	45.94

Balance on the cash account

	£
Opening balance	84,579.77
Cash book receipts total	70,710.14
Cash book payments total	(81,537.46)
Cash book balance	73,752.45

(b) **Main ledger accounts**

Sales ledger control account

		£			£
24/6	Balance b/d	312,465.99	30/6	Cash book receipts	69,127.69
			30/6	Cash book receipts – discount	460.81

Mail order sales account

		£			£
			24/6	Balance b/d	26,578.46
			30/6	Cash book receipts	1,318.73

VAT control account

		£			£
30/6	Cash book payments	23,664.67	24/6	Balance b/d	29,375.32
			30/6	Cash book receipts	263.72

Discount allowed account

		£		£
24/6	Balance b/d	4,627.56		
30/6	Cash book receipts	460.81		

Purchases ledger control account

		£			£
30/6	Cash book payments	8,550.14	24/6	Balance b/d	25,476.34
30/6	Cash book payments – discount	45.94			

Salaries account

		£		£
24/6	Balance b/d	105,374.36		
30/6	Cash book payments	48,995.63		

Electricity account

		£			£
24/6	Balance b/d	1,496.57			
30/6	Cash book payments	135.98			

Telephone account

		£			£
24/6	Balance b/d	967.47			
30/6	Cash book payments	191.04			

Discount received account

		£			£
			24/6	Balance b/d	336.58
			30/6	Cash book payments	45.94

(c)

FINANCIAL BANK PLC

CONFIDENTIAL

467 HIGH STREET
TAUNTON
TA1 9WE
Telephone
01832 722098

Account **CURRENT** Sheet 455

Account name **NATURAL PRODUCTS LIMITED**

20X1 Statement date: 30 JUNE 20X1 Account Number 34786695

Date	Details		Withdrawals (£)	Deposits (£)	Balance (£)
27 JUN	Balance from sheet 454				11,305.11
27 JUN	MEGASTORES PLC	CHAPS		11,755.25 ✓	
	COUNTER CREDIT 591			13,604.01	
	COUNTER CREDIT 592			112.13	
	374		127.09		
	376	DD	5,955.80		
	ENGLISH ELECTRIC		163.17 ✓		30,530.44
28 JUN	COUNTER CREDIT 593			11,655.24	
	COUNTER CREDIT 594			683.11	
	COUNTER CREDIT 595			112.19	
	372		87.93		
	389	DD	325.99 ✓		
	ENGLISH TELECOM		229.24 ✓		42,337.82
29 JUN	COUNTER CREDIT 596			325.11	
	COUNTER CREDIT 597			60,331.90	
	391		2,112.16 ✓		
	382		331.80		
	FREEMAN FOODS GRP	CHAPS		14,776.04 ✓	
	COUNTER CREDIT 598			15,685.23 ✓	
	COUNTER CREDIT 599			394.51 ✓	
	COUNTER CREDIT 600			91.71 ✓	
	394		338.11 ✓		
	395		500.00 ✓		
	386		441.09		
	388		111.94		130,107.22
30 JUN	COUNTER CREDIT 601			6,650.28 ✓	
	COUNTER CREDIT 602			118.45 ✓	
	381		117.54		
	384		3,785.60		
	387		785.11		
	390		683.85 ✓		
	393		1,253.98 ✓		
	399		175.10		
	COUNTER CREDIT 603			12,223.81 ✓	
	COUNTER CREDIT 604			622.18 ✓	142,920.76

key SO Standing order DD Direct debit CP Card purchase AC Automated cash OD Overdrawn
CHAPS Clearing House Automated Payments System BACS Bankers Automated Clearing Service

CONTROL ACCOUNTS AND RECONCILIATIONS OF THE SALES AND PURCHASE LEDGER ACCOUNTS

27 FINAL ACCOUNTS

PURCHASE LEDGER CONTROL ACCOUNT

	Add/Subtract	£
Total from list of balances		52,750
Adjustment for (a)	Subtract	8,370
Adjustment for (b)	Subtract	540
Adjustment for (c)	Add	750
Adjustment for (d)	Add	462
Adjustment for (e)	Add	1,902
Adjustment for (f)	Add	540
Revised total to agree with PLCA		47,494

28 FINAL ACCOUNTS (2)

SALES LEDGER CONTROL ACCOUNT

	Add/Subtract	£
Total from list of balances		31,820
Adjustment for (a)	Subtract	73
Adjustment for (b)	Add	280
Adjustment for (c)	Subtract	5,542
Adjustment for (d)	Add	3,090
Adjustment for (e)	Add	935
Adjustment for (f)	Add	450
Revised total to agree with SLCA		30,960

29 BASIL SPENCE

(a) **Subsidiary ledger – sales ledger**

N Pevsner

	£		£
b/d	5,700	c/d	5,850
Sales	150		
	5,850		5,850
b/d	5,850		

R Hackney

	£		£
b/d	5,823	Cash	5,700
Sales	5,280	Bad debt	123
		c/d	5,280
	─────		─────
	11,103		11,103
	─────		─────
b/d	5,280		

Prince of Wales Hotel

	£		£
b/d	5,826	Cash	5,826
Sales	4,995	c/d	4,995
	─────		─────
	10,821		10,821
	─────		─────
b/d	4,995		

Subsidiary ledger – purchases ledger

E Lutyens

	£		£
Cash	2,700	b/d	5,481
c/d	5,631	Purchases	2,850
	─────		─────
	8,331		8,331
	─────		─────
		b/d	5,631

M Hutchinson

	£		£
Cash	150	b/d	5,553
c/d	7,458	Purchases	2,055
	─────		─────
	7,608		7,608
	─────		─────
		b/d	7,458

H Falkner

	£		£
Cash	2,469	b/d	5,559
c/d	6,450	Purchases	3,360
	8,919		8,919
		b/d	6,450

(b) **Sales ledger control account**

	£		£
b/d	17,349	Cash	11,526
Sales	10,425	Bad debts expense written off – R Hackney	123
		c/d	16,125
	27,774		27,774
b/d	16,125		

Purchases ledger control account

	£		£
Cash	5,319	b/d	16,593
c/d	19,539	Purchases	8,265
	24,858		24,858
		b/d	19,539

(c) **Bad debts expense**

	£		£
Sales ledger control account (written-off – Hackney)	123		

(d)

List of debtors	£	List of creditors	£
N Pevsner	5,850	E Lutyens	5,631
R Hackney	5,280	M Hutchinson	7,458
Prince of Wales Hotel	4,995	H Falkner	6,450
	16,125		19,539

30 BOOKS OF A BUSINESS

(a) Purchases ledger control account

	£		£
Cash paid	47,028	b/d	5,926
Purchases returns account	202	Purchases (total from PDB)	47,713
Discounts received account	867		
Sales ledger control account (contra)	75		
c/d (bal fig)	5,467		
	53,639		53,639

(b) Sales ledger control account

	£		£
b/d	10,268	Bank account	69,872
Sales (total from SDB)	71,504	Bad debts account	96
		Sales returns account (total from SRDB)	358
		Discounts allowed (total from discount column in CB)	1,435
		Purchases ledger control account (contra)	75
		c/d (bal fig)	9,936
	81,772		81,772

31 BIRKETT

(a) **Purchases ledger control account**

	£		£
Cash (2)	1,800	Draft bal b/d	97,186
Contra – sales ledger (3)	1,386	Purchases day book	
Bal c/d	100,000	undercast (1)	6,000
	103,186		103,186
		Adjusted bal b/d	100,000

(b) **Reconciliation with list of balances**

	£
Total per list of balances	96,238
Debit balance extracted as a credit (4)	(80)
Balance omitted (5)	3,842
Adjusted balance per control account	100,000

32 ROBIN & CO

(a) **Sales ledger control account**

		£			£
30 Sep	b/d	3,825	30 Sep	Bad debts account (2)	400
				Purchases ledger control account (4)	70
				Discount allowed (5)	140
				c/d	3,215
		3,825			3,825
1 Oct	b/d	3,215			

(b) **List of sales ledger balances**

	£
Original total	3,362
Add: Debit balances previously omitted (1)	103
	3,465
Less: Item posted twice to Sparrow's account (3)	(250)
Amended total agreeing with balance on sales ledger control account	3,215

PRACTICE ANSWERS: SECTION 2

33 ERRORS

(a)

Account	Amount £	Debit ✓	Credit ✓
Bad debt expense	800	✓	
Sales ledger control	800		✓

(b)

Account	Amount £	Debit ✓	Credit ✓
Purchases ledger control	240	✓	
Sales ledger control	240		✓

(c)

Account	Amount £	Debit ✓	Credit ✓
Discount allowed	100	✓	
Sales ledger control	100		✓

34 PURCHASES LEDGER CONTROL ACCOUNT

(a)

Account	Amount £	Debit ✓	Credit ✓
Purchase ledger control	1,000	✓	
Purchases	1,000		✓

(b)

Account	Amount £	Debit ✓	Credit ✓
Purchases ledger control	9	✓	
Discount received	9		✓

(c)

Account	Amount £	Debit ✓	Credit ✓
Purchases ledger control	300	✓	
Sales ledger control	300		✓

CORRECTION OF ERRORS AND THE SUSPENSE ACCOUNT

35 PERCY

(a) **Journal**

Account	Amount £	Dr ✓	Cr ✓
Bad debt	500	✓	
Sales ledger control account	500		✓
Bad debt	715	✓	
Sales ledger control account	715		✓

(b) **Journal**

Account	Amount £	Dr ✓	Cr ✓
Motor repairs	880	✓	
Suspense	880		✓

(c) **Journal**

Account	Amount £	Dr ✓	Cr ✓
Closing stock – balance sheet	31,610	✓	
Closing stock – P&L	31,610		✓

(d) **Journal**

Account	Amount £	Dr ✓	Cr ✓
VAT	5,000	✓	
Suspense	5,000		✓
VAT	5,000	✓	
Suspense	5,000		✓

PRACTICE ANSWERS: SECTION 2

36 JACKSONS

Extract from extended trial balance

	Ledger balances		Adjustments	
	Dr £	Cr £	Dr £	Cr £
Accruals		365		
Bank	4,300			1,600
Closing stock – balance sheet			17,700	
Closing stock – P&L account				17,700
Depreciation charge				
Bad debts			220	
Loan		4,000		
Loan interest	240			
Plant and machinery – accumulated depreciation		22,000		
Sales		210,000		
Sales ledger control account	24,500		400	220
Suspense		1,200	1,600	400
VAT		5,600		

37 HERMES DELIVERIES

(a) **Journal**

Account	Amount £	Dr ✓	Cr ✓
Stationery	275	✓	
Suspense	275		✓

(b) **Journal**

Account	Amount £	Dr ✓	Cr ✓
Closing stock – balance sheet	34,962	✓	
Closing stock – P&L account	34,962		✓

(c) **Journal**

Account	Amount £	Dr ✓	Cr ✓
Bad debt	210	✓	
Sales ledger control account	210		✓

KAPLAN PUBLISHING

(d) **Journal**

Account	Amount £	Dr ✔	Cr ✔
Suspense	6,400	✔	
VAT	6,400		✔
Suspense	6,400	✔	
VAT	6,400		✔

38 EVANS AND CO

(a)

	£	Debit	Credit
Capital	50,000		50,000
Purchases	83,468	83,468	
Revenue	159,407		159,407
Purchase Returns	2,693		2,693
Sales Returns	3,090	3,090	
SLCA	25,642	25,642	
PLCA	31,007		31,007
Drawings	25,500	25,500	
Machinery – Cost	45,900	45,900	
Machinery – Accumulated Depreciation	15,925		15,925
Rent and Rates	15,600	15,600	
Light and Heat	2,466	2,466	
Motor Expenses	2,603	2,603	
Loan	12,500		12,500
Interest	1,250	1,250	
Discounts received	400		400
Bad debts	1,300	1,300	
Accruals	2,572		2,572
Salaries	77,921	77,921	
Bank overdraft	3,876		3,876
Suspense			6,360
Totals		**284,740**	**284,740**

PRACTICE ANSWERS: SECTION 2

(b)

		Amount £	Dr ✓	Cr ✓
(i)	Drawings	1,000	✓	
	Salaries	1,000		✓
(ii)	Suspense	280	✓	
	Purchases	280		✓
(iii)	Suspense	70	✓	
	VAT	70		✓
(iv)	Suspense	3,175	✓	
	Bank	3,175		✓
	Suspense	3,175	✓	
	Bank	3,175		✓
(v)	Electricity	340	✓	
	Suspense	340		✓

39 RACHEL EDMUNDSON

(a)

	£	Debit	Credit
Accruals	4,820		4,820
Prepayments	2,945	2,945	
Motor expenses	572	572	
Administration expenses	481	481	
Light and heat	1,073	1,073	
Revenue	48,729		48,729
Purchases	26,209	26,209	
SLCA	5,407	5,407	
PLCA	3,090		3,090
Rent	45	45	
Purchase returns	306		306
Discounts allowed	567	567	
Capital	10,000		10,000
Loan	15,000		15,000
Interest paid	750	750	
Drawings	4,770	4,770	
Motor Vehicles – cost	19,000	19,000	
Motor Vehicle – accumulated depreciation	2,043		2,043
VAT control account	2,995		2,995
Wages	20,000	20,000	
Suspense account		**5,164**	
Totals		**86,983**	**86,983**

(b)

		Dr £	Cr £
(i)	Suspense	5,000	
	Capital		5,000
(ii)	Suspense	385	
	Sales ledger control		385
(iii)	VAT	193	
	Suspense		193
(iv)	Rent	4,500	
	Suspense		4,500
	Rent	4,500	
	Suspense		4,500
(v)	Electricity	1,356	
	Suspense		1,356

DEPRECIATION OF FIXED ASSETS

40   SOUTHGATE TRADING

Description	Acquisition date	Cost £	Depreciation £	Net Book value £
Computer equipment				
Server main office	30/09/X6	2,800.00		
Year-end 31/03/X7			840.00	1,960.00
Year end 31/03/X8			840.00	1,120.00
Year end 31/03/X9			**840.00**	**280.00**
HP printer 65438LKR	**28/03/X9**	**775.00**		
Year end 31/03/X9			**232.50**	**542.50**
MOTOR VEHICLES				
AB08 DRF	01/04/X6	12,000.00		
Year end 31/03/X7			3,000.00	9,000.00
Year end 31/03/X8			2,250.00	6,750.00
Year end 31/03/X9			**1,687.50**	**5,062.50**
AB 07 FRP	31/01/X8	9,600.00		
Year end 31/03/X8			2,400.00	7,200.00
Year end 31/03/X9			**1,800.00**	**5,400.00**

41 NON-CURRENT ASSET LEDGERS

Vehicles at cost

Balance b/d	10,000		
Bank	7,500	Balance c/d	17,500
	17,500		17,500

Vehicles accumulated depreciation

		Balance b/d	3,000
Balance c/d	4,500	Depreciation charge	1,500
	4,500		4,500

Depreciation charge

Balance b/d	1,000		
Vehicles accumulated depreciation	1,500	Income statement	2,500
	2,500		2,500

42 KATY'S CAKES

Equipment at cost

Balance b/d	6,200		
Bank	8,500	Balance c/d	14,700
	14,700		14,700

Equipment accumulated depreciation

		Balance b/d	1,900
		Depreciation charge – existing	430
Balance c/d	3,180	Depreciation charge – new	850
	3,180		3,180

Depreciation charge

Balance b/d	3,000		
Depreciation charge – existing	430		
Depreciation charge – new	850	Income statement	4,280
	4,280		4,280

(d) **Capital Expenditure**

	Tick
The money spent on the purchase of non-current assets	✓

43 MEAD

Motor car – cost account

	£		£
20X3		20X3	
1 Jan Purchase ledger control	12,000	31 Dec Balance c/d	12,000
20X4		20X4	
1 Jan Balance b/d	12,000	31 Dec Balance c/d	12,000
20X5		20X5	
1 Jan Balance b/d	12,000	31 Dec Balance c/d	12,000
20X6			
1 Jan Balance b/d	12,000		

Annual depreciation charge $= \dfrac{12{,}000 - 2{,}400}{4}$

$= £2{,}400$

Motor car – accumulated depreciation account

	£		£
20X3		20X3	
31 Dec Balance c/d	2,400	31 Dec Depreciation expense	2,400
20X4		20X4	
31 Dec Balance c/d	4,800	1 Jan Balance b/d	2,400
		31 Dec Depreciation expense	2,400
	4,800		4,800
20X5		20X5	
31 Dec Balance c/d	7,200	1 Jan Balance b/d	4,800
		31 Dec Depreciation expense	2,400
	7,200		7,200
		20X6	
		1 Jan Balance b/d	7,200

Depreciation expense account

	£		£
20X3		20X3	
31 Dec Motor car accumulated depreciation	2,400	31 Dec P&L a/c	2,400
20X4		20X4	
31 Dec Motor car accumulated depreciation	2,400	31 Dec P&L a/c	2,400
20X5		20X5	
31 Dec Motor car accumulated depreciation	2,400	31 Dec P&L a/c	2,400

44 S TELFORD

(a) **Straight line method**

$$\text{Annual depreciation} = \frac{\text{Cost} - \text{Scrap value}}{\text{Estimated life}}$$

$$= \frac{£6,000 - £1,000}{8 \text{ years}}$$

$$= £625 \text{ pa}$$

Machine account

	£		£
Year 1:			
Cost	6,000		

Provision for depreciation

	£		£
Year 1:		**Year 1:**	
Balance c/d	625	Depreciation expense	625
Year 2:		**Year 2:**	
		Balance b/d	625
Balance c/d	1,250	Depreciation expense	625
	1,250		1,250
Year 3:		**Year 3:**	
		Balance b/d	1,250
Balance c/d	1,875	Depreciation expense	625
	1,875		1,875
		Year 4:	
		Balance b/d	1,875

Balance sheet extract:

		Cost	Accumulated depreciation	Net book value
		£	£	£
Fixed asset:				
Year 1	Machine	6,000	625	5,375
Year 2	Machine	6,000	1,250	4,750
Year 3	Machine	6,000	1,875	4,125

(b) **Reducing balance method**

		£
Cost		6,000
Year 1	Depreciation 20% × £6,000	1,200
		4,800
Year 2	Depreciation 20% × £4,800	960
		3,840
Year 3	Depreciation 20% × £3,840	768
Net book value		3,072

45 HILTON

(a) **Machinery**

Workings

	Chopper	Mincer	Stuffer	Total
	£	£	£	£
Cost	4,000	6,000	8,000	18,000
Depreciation 20X6	(1,000)			(1,000)
Depreciation 20X7	(1,000)	(1,500)		(2,500)
Depreciation 20X8	(1,000)	(1,500)	(2,000)	(4,500)
NBV at 31 Dec 20X8	1,000	3,000	6,000	10,000

Machinery

	£		£
20X6		**20X6**	
Cash – chopper	4,000	Balance c/d	4,000
20X7		**20X7**	
Balance b/d	4,000		
Cash – mincer	6,000	Balance c/d	10,000
	10,000		10,000
20X8		**20X8**	
Balance b/d	10,000		
Cash – stuffer	8,000	Balance c/d	18,000
	18,000		18,000
20X9			
Balance b/d	18,000		

Accumulated depreciation (machinery)

	£		£
20X6		20X6	
Balance c/d	1,000	Depreciation expense (25% × £4,000)	1,000
20X7		20X7	
Balance c/d	3,500	Balance b/d	1,000
		Depreciation expense (25% × £10,000)	2,500
	3,500		3,500
20X8		20X8	
Balance c/d	8,000	Balance b/d	3,500
		Depreciation expense (25% × £18,000)	4,500
	8,000		8,000
		20X9	
		Balance b/d	8,000

Depreciation expense (machinery)

	£		£
20X6		20X6	
Accumulated depreciation	1,000	Profit and loss account	1,000
20X7		20X7	
Accumulated depreciation	2,500	Profit and loss account	2,500
20X8		20X8	
Accumulated depreciation	4,500	Profit and loss account	4,500

(b) **Vehicles**

Workings

	Metro £	Transit £	Astra £	Total £
Cost	3,200	6,000	4,200	13,400
Depreciation 20X6	(1,280)			(1,280)
NBV 31.12.X6	1,920			
Depreciation 20X7	(768)	(2,400)		(3,168)
NBV 31.12.X7	1,152	3,600		
Depreciation 20X8	(461)	(1,440)	(1,680)	(3,581)
Net book value at 31 Dec 20X8	691	2,160	2,520	5,371

Motor vehicles

	£		£
20X6		20X6	
Cash – Metro	3,200	Balance c/d	3,200
20X7		20X7	
Balance b/d	3,200		
Cash – Transit	6,000	Balance c/d	9,200
	9,200		9,200
20X8		20X8	
Balance b/d	9,200		
Cash – Astra	4,200	Balance c/d	13,400
	13,400		13,400
20X9			
Balance b/d	13,400		

Accumulated depreciation (motor vehicles)

	£		£
20X6		**20X6**	
		Depreciation expense	
Balance c/d	1,280	(40% × £3,200)	1,280
20X7		**20X7**	
Balance c/d	4,448	Balance b/d	1,280
		Depreciation expense	
		(40% × (£9,200 − £1,280))	3,168
	4,448		4,448
20X8		**20X8**	
Balance c/d	8,029	Balance b/d	4,448
		Depreciation expense	
		(40% × (£13,400 − £4,448))	3,581
	8,029		8,029
		20X9	
		Balance b/d	8,029

Depreciation expense (motor vehicles)

	£		£
20X6		**20X6**	
Accumulated depreciation	1,280	Profit and loss account	1,280
20X7		**20X7**	
Accumulated depreciation	3,168	Profit and loss account	3,168
20X8		**20X8**	
Accumulated depreciation	3,581	Profit and loss account	3,581

46 INFORTEC COMPUTERS

	£
Depreciation for vehicle sold 1 March 20X3	900
Depreciation for vehicle purchased 1 June 20X3	1,000
Depreciation for vehicle purchased 1 September 20X3	600
Depreciation for other vehicles owned during the year	2,080
Total depreciation for the year ended 30 November 20X3	4,580

ACCRUALS AND PREPAYMENTS

47 ACCRUALS AND PREPAYMENTS (1)

(a) **Administration expenses**

Bank	7,190	Balance b/d	790
		Balance c/d	1,800
		Income statement	4,600
	7,190		7,190

(b) **Selling expenses**

Balance b/d	475	Income statement	9,275
Bank	7,900		
Balance c/d	900		
	9,275		9,275

(c) **Extract** from trial balance as at 31 March 20X1.

Account		Dr	Cr
	£	£	£
Accruals			900
Capital	6,000		6,000
Wages & Salaries	850	850	
Selling expenses		9,275	
Drawings	11,000	11,000	
Administration expenses		4,600	
Interest received	70		70
Machinery at cost	5,600	5,600	
Machinery accumulated depreciation	4,200		4,200
Prepayments		1,800	

48 ACCRUALS AND PREPAYMENTS (2)

(a) Electricity expenses

Bank	10,539	Balance b/d	2,815
		Balance c/d	1,572
		Income statement	6,152
	10,539		10,539

(b) Rental expenses

Balance b/d	6,250	Income statement	75,000
Bank	62,500		
Balance c/d	6,250		
	75,000		75,000

(c) Extract from trial balance as at 31 March 20X6

Account		Dr	Cr
	£	£	£
Accruals			6,250
Accumulated depreciation – Office equipment	17,921		17,921
Depreciation charge	3,805	3,805	
Drawings	22,400	22,400	
Electricity		6,152	
Interest received	129		129
Office Equipment – cost	42,784	42,784	
Rental		75,000	
Stationery	2,800	2,800	
Prepayments		1,572	

49 SIOBHAN

Rent payable

	£		£
Cash paid	15,000	P&L account	12,000
		Bal c/d	3,000
	15,000		15,000
Bal b/d (prepayment)	3,000		

Gas

	£		£
Cash paid	840	P&L account	1,440
Bal c/d	600		
	1,440		1,440
		Bal b/d (accrual)	600

Advertising

	£		£
Cash	3,850	P&L account	3,350
		Bal c/d	500
	3,850		3,850
Bal b/d (prepayment)	500		

Bank interest

	£		£
Cash	28	P&L account	96
Cash	45		
Bal c/d (⅓ × 69)	23		
	96		96
		Bal b/d (accrual)	23

Rates

	£		£
Brought forward		P&L account	11,300
(prepayment $3/6 \times 4{,}800$)	2,400		
Cash	5,600		
Bal c/d ($3/6 \times 6{,}600$)	3,300		
	11,300		11,300
		Bal b/d (accrual)	3,300

Rent receivable

	£		£
Brought forward		Cash	250
(debtor = accrued income)	125	Cash	600
P&L account (W)	575		
Bal c/d ($3/12 \times 600$)	150		
	850		850
		Bal b/d	
		(creditor = deferred income)	150

Working:

Profit and loss account credit for rent receivable

	£
1 January 20X4 – 31 March 20X4 ($3/6 \times 250$)	125
1 April 20X4 – 31 December 20X4 ($9/12 \times 600$)	450
	575

50   A CREW

Stationery

		£			£
31 Dec	Balance per trial balance	560	31 Dec	P&L account	545
			31 Dec	C/f (prepayment)	15
		560			560
1 Jan	Brought forward	15			

Rent

		£			£
31 Dec	Balance per trial balance	900	31 Dec	P&L account	1,200
31 Dec	Carried forward (accrual)	300			
		1,200			1,200
			1 Jan	Brought forward	300

Rates

		£			£
31 Dec	Balance per trial balance	380	31 Dec	P&L account	310
			31 Dec	C/f (prepayment)	70
		380			380
1 Jan	Brought forward	70			

Lighting and heating

		£			£
31 Dec	Balance per trial balance	590	31 Dec	P&L account	605
31 Dec	Carried forward (accrual)	15			
		605			605
			1 Jan	Brought forward	15

Insurance

	£		£
31 Dec Balance per trial balance	260	31 Dec P&L account	190
		31 Dec C/f (prepayment)	70
	260		260
1 Jan Brought forward	70		

Wages and salaries

	£		£
31 Dec Balance per trial balance	2,970	31 Dec P&L account	2,970

51 A METRO

Motor tax and insurance

	£		£
Brought forward	570	P&L account (W2)	2,205
Cash		Carried forward (W1)	835
1 April	420		
1 May	1,770		
1 July	280		
	3,040		3,040
Brought forward	835		

Workings:

(W1) Prepayment at the end of the year

	£
Motor tax on six vans paid 1 April 20X0 ($3/12 \times 420$)	105
Insurance on ten vans paid 1 May 20X0 ($4/12 \times 1,770$)	590
Motor tax on four vans paid 1 July 20X0 ($6/12 \times 280$)	140
Total prepayment	835

(W2) Profit and loss charge for the year

There is no need to calculate this as it is the balancing figure, but it could be calculated as follows.

	£
Prepayment	570
Motor tax ($9/12 \times 420$)	315
Insurance ($8/12 \times 1,770$)	1,180
Motor tax ($6/12 \times 280$)	140
Profit and loss charge	2,205

BAD DEBTS

52 PUTNEY

Sales (debtors) ledger control account

	£		£
Balance b/d	34,500	Cash received	229,900
Credit sales (β)	278,090	Contra	1,200
		Discounts allowed	17,890
		Bad debts	18,600
		Balance c/d	45,000
	312,590		312,590
Balance b/f	45,000		

Total sales = Credit sales + Cash sales

= £278,090 + £24,000

= **£302,090**

Note:

(i) Discounts received are relevant to the payables ledger control account.

(ii) The provision for doubtful debt does not affect the SLCA.

53 PURDEY

Debtors ledger control account

	£		£
Balance b/d	84,700	Contra with creditors ledger control account	5,000
Credit sales	644,000	Bad debts	4,300
		Discounts allowed	30,780
		Cash received from credit customers	595,000
		Balance c/d	93,620
	728,700		728,700

Note:

(i) The double entry for a contra is Dr creditors ledger control account and Cr debtors ledger control account.

(ii) Discounts received are relevant to creditors not debtors.

(iii) Cash sales should not feature in the debtors ledger control account.

(iv) The provision for doubtful debt does not affect the DLCA.

54 BORIS

Debtors/sales ledger control account

	£		£
Balance b/d	12,000		
Sales	125,000	Cash received	115,500
		Bad debts	7,100
		Balance c/d	14,400
	137,000		137,000
Balance b/d	**14,400**		

PRACTICE ANSWERS: SECTION 2

55 FAUNTLEROY

Debtors/sales ledger control account

	£		£
Balance b/d (β)	108,567	Bad debts	3,200
Credit sales	6,000,000	Contra (PLCA)	2,700
		Cash received	5,360,000
Increase in allowance	2,333	Balance c/d	745,000
	6,110,900		6,110,900

56 TIPTON

Debtors/sales ledger control account

	£		£
Balance b/d	10,000	Receipts	90,000
Sales	100,000	Discounts allowed	800
		Balance c/d	19,200
	110,000		110,000
Balance b/d	19,200		

57 A

Receivables

	$		$
Balance b/d	37,500	Discounts allowed	15,750
Sales (credit)	357,500	Bad debts written off	10,500
		Bank (β)	**329,750**
		Balance c/d	39,000
	395,000		395,000

FINAL ACCOUNTS OF A SOLE TRADER

58 PG TRADING

(a)

PG Trading

Profit and loss account for the year ended 30 September 20X8

	£	£
Sales		170,850
Opening stock	17,700	
Purchases	98,000	
Closing stock	(19,500)	
Cost of goods sold		(96,200)
Gross profit		74,650
Less:		
Depreciation charge	7,100	
Discounts allowed	1,350	
General expenses	26,100	
Rent	7,300	
Wages	8,500	
Total expenses		(50,350)
Net profit for the year		24,300

(b) (ii) Current assets

59 STOCK TRADING

(a) **Stock Trading**

Profit and loss account for the year ended 30 September 20X9

	£	£
Sales (W)		162,500
Opening stock	3,450	
Purchases	125,000	
Closing stock	(7,850)	
Cost of goods sold		(120,600)
Gross profit		41,900
Add:		
Discounts received	900	
Disposal	450	
Total Sundry Income		1,350
Less:		
Depreciation charge	1,600	
Discounts allowed	345	
General expenses	2,950	
Rent	5,250	
Bad debts	295	
Wages	24,000	
Total expenses		(34,440)
Net profit for the year		8,810

Working:

	£
Sales per TB	164,000
Sales returns per TB	(1,500)
	162,500

(b) (ii) As a deduction from capital

60 TONY BROWN

(a) **Profit and loss account for the year ended 31 March 20X7**

	£	£
Sales		80,000
Opening stock	1,500	
Purchases	34,500	
Closing stock	(1,620)	
Cost of goods sold		(34,380)
Gross profit		45,620
Less:		
Repairs and maintenance	1,520	
Motor vehicle running costs	3,450	
Insurances	1,250	
Office expenses	600	
Wages	8,000	
Total expenses		(14,280)
Profit for the year		30,800

(b) **Balance sheet as at 31 March 20X7**

	£	£
Fixed assets		
Motor vehicles		17,000
Tools and equipment		19,600
Office equipment		4,000
		40,600
Current assets		
Stock	1,620	
Trade debtors	3,600	
Cash at bank	1,280	
Cash in hand	100	
	6,600	
Creditors due within one year		
Trade creditors	2,100	
VAT due to HMRC	800	
	2,900	
Net current assets		3,700
Total assets less current liabilities		44,300
Long term liabilities		
Bank loan		4,500
Net assets		39,800
Financed by:		
Capital		30,000
Profit for the year		30,800
Drawings		(21,000)
		39,800

61 JOHN RISDON

J Risdon profit and loss account for year ended 31 March 2007

	£	£
Sales		84,500
Opening stock	1,750	
Add purchases	38,100	
Less closing stocks	(1,850)	
Cost of goods sold		(38,000)
Gross Profit		46,500
Expenses		
Repairs and Maintenance	1,750	
Motor Vehicle Running Cost	4,100	
Insurance	1,400	
Office Expenses	700	
Wages	8,750	
		(16,700)
Net profit for year		29,800

Balance Sheet as at 31 March 2007

	£	£
Fixed Assets		
Tools and Equipment		20,000
Motor Vehicles		18,500
Office Equipment		5,000
		43,500
Current Assets		
Stocks	1,850	
Debtors	4,100	
Bank	4,000	
Cash	450	
	10,400	
Less Current Liabilities		
Creditors	2,600	
VAT	1,000	
	3,600	
Net Current Assets		6,800
Total Assets Less Current Liabilities		50,300
Less Long Term Liabilities		
Loan		6,500
		43,800
Financed by:		
Capital		36,000
Add profit for year		29,800
Less Drawings		(22,000)
		43,800

62 ANDREW FEWSTER

Andrew Fewster profit and loss account for year ended 31 March 20X7

	£	£
Sales		86,500
Opening stock	1,950	
Add Purchases	39,500	
Less closing stock	(2,150)	
Cost of goods sold		(39,300)
Gross Profit		47,200
Expenses		
Repairs to Hallways	1,950	
Motor Vehicle Running Costs	4,250	
Insurance (1850 – 250)	1,600	
Office Expenses (950 +50)	1,000	
Wages	9,200	
Depreciation Motor Vehicles	5,625	
Depreciation Tools & Equipment	5,250	
Depreciation Office Equipment	1,375	
		(30,250)
Net profit for year		16,950

Balance Sheet as at 31 March 20X7

	£	£
Fixed Assets		
Motor Vehicle		16,875
Tools & Equipment		15,750
Office Equipment		4,125
		36,750
Current Assets		
Stocks	2,150	
Debtors	5,500	
Pre-Payments	250	
Bank	1,000	
Cash	200	
	9,100	
Less Current Liabilities		
Creditors	2,950	
Accruals	50	
VAT	1,400	
	4,400	
Net current assets		4,700
Total assets less current liabilities		41,450
Less Long Term Liabilities		
Bank loan		10,500
		30,950
Financed by:		
Capital		37,500
Net profit for year		16,950
Less drawings		(23,500)
		30,950